Library of
Davidson College

PUBLIC OPINION AND
FOREIGN POLICY

PUBLIC OPINION
AND
FOREIGN POLICY

By LESTER MARKEL
AND
HANSON W. BALDWIN MARTIN KRIESBERG
ARNALDO CORTESI CABELL PHILLIPS
W. PHILLIPS DAVISON JAMES RESTON
C. D. JACKSON SHEPARD STONE

Essay Index Reprint Series

BOOKS FOR LIBRARIES PRESS
FREEPORT, NEW YORK

Copyright, 1949, by Council on Foreign Relations, Inc.

Reprinted 1972 by arrangement.

Library of Congress Cataloging in Publication Data

Markel, Lester, 1894-
  Public opinion and foreign policy.

  (Essay index reprint series)
  Reprint of the 1949 ed.
  1. United States--Foreign relations--20th century--Addresses, essays, lectures. 2. Public opinion--United States--Addresses, essays, lectures. I. Title.
E744.M355 1972   327.73   78-167404
ISBN 0-8369-7242-2

PRINTED IN THE UNITED STATES OF AMERICA

COUNCIL ON FOREIGN RELATIONS

OFFICERS AND DIRECTORS

R. C. LEFFINGWELL
Chairman of the Board

ALLEN W. DULLES
President

ISAIAH BOWMAN
Vice-President

FRANK ALTSCHUL
Secretary

CLARENCE E. HUNTER
Treasurer

WALTER H. MALLORY
Executive Director

HAMILTON FISH ARMSTRONG
WILLIAM A. M. BURDEN
JOHN W. DAVIS
LEWIS W. DOUGLAS
STEPHEN DUGGAN
THOMAS K. FINLETTER

GEORGE O. MAY
PHILIP D. REED
WINFIELD W. RIEFLER
WHITNEY H. SHEPARDSON
MYRON C. TAYLOR
JOHN H. WILLIAMS

HENRY M. WRISTON

COMMITTEE ON STUDIES

HENRY M. WRISTON
Chairman

HAMILTON FISH ARMSTRONG
ISAIAH BOWMAN
ALLEN W. DULLES
GRAYSON KIRK

STACY MAY
WINFIELD W. RIEFLER
BEARDSLEY RUML
JOHN H. WILLIAMS

The authors of books published under the auspices of the Council on Foreign Relations are responsible for their statements of fact and expressions of opinion. The Council is responsible only for determining that they should be presented to the public.

FOREWORD

IN March 1947 a group of Council members met to organize a study of public opinion in its relation to United States foreign policy. Three facts gave point to the study: (1) the growing power of propaganda as a factor in international relations, (2) changes in the techniques of instructing and influencing public opinion through new media of mass communication, and (3) the uncertainty of American policy with respect to public opinion operations both at home and abroad.

Public opinion is vital but elusive, difficult to capture and record in books and documents. So the Council first brought together a small group of its members who were knowledgeable in the fields of mass communication and foreign policy to advise on the project, to give direction to the study and to discuss major issues. Lester Markel, Sunday editor of the *New York Times,* was asked to serve as chairman. At a number of meetings, officials of the U. S. Department of State and the Department of Army explained their activities in the field of public opinion. At other meetings Washington correspondents described and commented on the handling of press relations by the White House and the State Department.

Meanwhile, the process of collecting basic data had begun. For this purpose the Council enlisted the services of three scholars who had specialized in the psychology of American public opinion in its relation to the democratic process. They were W. Phillips Davison, editor of the *Public Opinion Quarterly;* Dr. Martin Kriesberg, of the Department of Political Science at the University of Michigan; and Avery Leiserson, Assistant Professor of Political Science at the University of Chicago. Only a part of their extensive memoranda appears in signed chapters in this book; a large part was pooled and has been drawn on freely by the other writers.

To supplement the research studies the Council asked for contributions from a number of journalists—Hanson W. Baldwin, Cabell Phillips, James Reston and Shepard Stone, all of the staff of the *New York Times,* and C. D. Jackson, Vice President of *Time,* Inc. In their chapters these authors have drawn upon rich stores of experience with public affairs and with the practical operation of the forces of public opinion.

The purpose of the group's discussions was to explore thoroughly the subject matter rather than to arrive at a set of conclusions or recommendations to which all, or a majority, could subscribe. Consequently, although the group found itself in general in accord with the views of the various authors, the latter bear sole responsibility for their opinions.

For valuable information on the state of public opinion abroad, and on the effectiveness of American information and propaganda activities in foreign countries, the authors gratefully acknowledge their indebtedness to a number of foreign correspondents of the American press. Their names and connections are given on a later page.

Valuable assistance in editing the manuscript and preparing it for publication was given by John Desmond and Daniel Schwarz of the staff of the *New York Times,* and by Byron Dexter, George S. Franklin, Jr. and Helena Stalson of the Council on Foreign Relations.

Dr. Henry M. Wriston, President of Brown University, helped to make this study possible by appointing Messrs. Davison, Kriesberg and Leiserson as President's Fellows. Financial aid was also supplied by the Carnegie Corporation.

Many minds have contributed to this study. But in a real

sense this is Lester Markel's book. Deeply concerned with the need, in this critical state of world affairs, for a better understanding both at home and abroad of the aims of American foreign policy, he first proposed that the Council undertake this study of the activities of the United States Government in the closely allied fields of information and propaganda. As chairman of the Council's study group he organized its discussions, he laid out writing assignments and skillfully edited the contributions of the various authors so as to give unity and coherence to the book. In addition, he has himself written the first and last chapters. His Introduction discusses the interdependence of public opinion and foreign policy, thus setting up a background for the chapters that follow. In the closing chapter he summarizes the findings of his collaborators and comes to grips with the tough question of leadership in the making of foreign policy.

PERCY W. BIDWELL
Director of Studies

Council on Foreign Relations
January 1949

ACKNOWLEDGMENTS

Acknowledgment is due the following foreign correspondents who contributed reports on the effectiveness of American information activities in foreign countries:

New York Times

George Axelsson
Milton Bracker
Arthur Brandel
Harold Callender
Delbert Clark
Clifton Daniel
Tillman Durdin
Frank M. Garcia
Carlos Griffin
Sydney Gruson
R. J. H. Johnston
John MacCormac
Lindesay Parrott
A. H. Ross
Dana Schmidt
A. C. Sedgwick

New York Herald Tribune

Ralph Chapman
Mac R. Johnson
Barrett McGurn

Time

Leo Hochstetter
William Johnson
Carl Mydans
Violet Price
William White

Columbia Broadcasting Company

William Costello
Stephen Laird
George Polk
David Schoenbrun

National Broadcasting Company

William Brooks
Henry Cassidy
George T. Folster
Edwin L. Haaker
Max Jordan
Merrill Mueller

CONTENTS

Foreword vii

INTRODUCTION

I. Opinion—A Neglected Instrument . . . 3
   By Lester Markel

PART ONE

FOREIGN POLICY AND OPINION AT HOME

II. Dark Areas of Ignorance 49
   By Martin Kriesberg

III. The Number One Voice 65
   By James Reston

IV. The Mirror Called Congress 78
   By Cabell Phillips

V. When the Big Guns Speak 97
   By Hanson W. Baldwin

VI. More Than Diplomacy 121
   By W. Phillips Davison

PART TWO

FOREIGN POLICY AND OPINION ABROAD

VII. Chart of the Cold War 143
   By Shepard Stone

VIII. Voices of America 156
   By W. Phillips Davison

IX. Assignment for The Press 180
  By C. D. Jackson

X. Two Vital Case Histories 197
  By Arnaldo Cortesi and "Observer"

CONCLUSION

XI. Opportunity or Disaster? 213
  By Lester Markel

INTRODUCTION

This chapter appraises the power of public opinion as an instrument of foreign policy; it points out our failure to use that instrument as it can and must be used; and outlines the problem of building a better opinion in its two aspects—first, at home, and second, abroad.

CHAPTER ONE

OPINION—A NEGLECTED INSTRUMENT

By Lester Markel

THE REASONS for this book are these:

that no American program, no plan for world order, can succeed unless it has the full support of public opinion, both at home and abroad;

that at home there are large areas of ignorance and prejudice about foreign affairs; abroad there are large segments of misinformation and suspicion about us;

that, unless we educate public opinion at home, we shall not be impelled to do the job in foreign policy that needs to be done; unless we make ourselves understood abroad, no matter how good our intentions, we shall fail.

The hopes for this book are these:

that it will help spread the conviction that a better informed opinion is vital to us;

that it will bring some light into the areas of information and propaganda—areas in which light is greatly needed;

that it will prove of some service to the makers of our foreign policy—in the White House, in Congress, in the State Department, especially among the people—in this task of enlightenment.

1. *Our New Role in the World*

These are the three overriding facts in today's world:

There is, first, the *unity of events.* We cannot thrust aside the world role which circumstance has assigned to us; we cannot escape our destiny; we are for all time de-isolated.

There is, second, the *speed of events*. Even though we are three thousand miles distant from the nearest coast of the old world, the currents of world affairs beat unceasingly on our shores.

There is, third, the *mass of events*. These are days when wars are fought and treaties are made, not between emperors or their mercenaries, but between peoples and peoples. The links are tightly joined; in war the front is everywhere, in peace all men are neighbors.

Thus what men think becomes of prime importance. Especially what *we* think and what others think of us. That can mean peace or disaster—for us and for the rest of the world.

We do not find it easy to grasp the urgency of that fact. Even in the pre-Politburo, pre-atomic age, understanding of foreign affairs for us was difficult and limited. In this period of a new type of diplomacy, of a new kind of world relations, of a new kind of world, perplexity is piled on perplexity.

Moreover, at this turning point in history, a new role is forced upon us. Suddenly we have been thrust into the very forefront of world affairs; we have become the nation to which the other nations look, for guidance, for succor—or for conflict.

We are not prepared for that role; our thinking has been outdistanced by the rush of history. Before we have been able to learn the techniques, or even the language of the new diplomacy, before we have been able fully to dispel the mists of isolationism that have clouded our vision for so many years, before we have been able to grow up internationally, the world is upon us and we must act.

We find ourselves engaged in a new kind of warfare, a battle for the minds of men. "Cold war," it is called, but it is waged with words of white heat. Our objective is to gain for American policies the support of public opinion both at home and abroad. Thus, that mysterious force, the viewpoint of the Man in the Street—on Main Street and on Wall Street, on Piccadilly, on the boulevards of Paris, on the Terazia in Belgrade, in Red Square in Moscow—is now our great concern.

Public opinion has become, for others if not for us, a powerful instrument of national policy. We, too, must learn to use it, but before we can use it effectively we must know more about it.

How well informed is American public opinion, particularly in the field of foreign affairs? What can be done to make it better informed? How effective is our propaganda abroad? What can be done to improve it?

This book is an attempt to give shape to these problems and to indicate possible approaches to their solution. It deals, in the main, with the operations of the government generally, and the State Department particularly, in the public opinion field.

At the outset it should be emphasized that the government alone cannot do the job—or even the major part of it. It should be recognized that, even if the government performed perfectly all its public opinion functions, there would be needed great improvements in our educational system and our press to bring about the kind of opinion we require. As one officer of the Department puts it:

> If the Department of State is to fully represent the American people, a far greater number of Americans than in the past must individually inform themselves on foreign affairs, think through their decisions, and make their views known.[1]

Yet it should be recognized also that the government itself has a large role to perform—and that is the special concern of this study.[2] The difficulties of the assignment at

---
[1] Francis Russell, "The Department of State and the Public," in Blair Bolles, "Who Makes Our Foreign Policy," Foreign Policy Association Headline Series, March-April 1947, p. 94.
[2] The other aspects of the problem of educating public opinion in the nation—notably those aspects that concern schools and colleges and the press

home are great, because of the areas of ignorance in the nation; abroad, they are even greater, because of the areas of misunderstanding in the world. Yet, despite the obstacles, the assignment must be fully undertaken.

2. End of the White-Shuttered Era

The visitor to the old State Department building—that tarnished wedding-cake structure opposite the White House—came away with one persistent impression: the array of white-slotted doors that seemed to stretch endlessly, as in a Chirico painting, through its corridors. If he were a frequent visitor, in search of information, these doors became symbolic. They seemed to be a combination of Victorian barrier and iron curtain—velvet prudishness and metallic sternness joined to hide what were presumably the most important secrets in the world. They were notice that, in the high-ceilinged rooms beyond, the great events in the making were matters for the High Priests and not for the Commoners.

The new State Department building, a mile away from the White House, is streamlined and business-like. Taken over from the army two years ago, it still has the khaki aroma and the khaki flavor about it. The doors are steel and modern and done in army brown; yet, figuratively, if not actually, many of the white shutters of the old building have been transported to the Department's new home. For there is still in the Department much of the feeling that foreign relations are its exclusive preserve and that therefore it need not give the people the facts.[3] And this same sentiment is found in other departments concerned with foreign policy.

—are dealt with in other places and other books, as the reader will readily recognize. The government's responsibility in that effort has had little attention, and that is the reason for this book.

[3] This criticism was made by Joseph M. Jones (*A Modern Foreign Policy for the United States,* New York, Macmillan, 1944, p. 46). Much of it is still valid.

There have been significant changes in this attitude—the trend is in the right direction—but there are still too many career diplomats who look upon themselves as Brahmins and upon fact-seekers as Untouchables; too many officials in high position who feel public opinion has no place in the frock-coated world in which both their bodies and their minds move; too many experts who, from their ivory towers, do not deign even to look down upon the Man in the Street to whom they must ultimately turn to implement their programs. These officials do not seem to realize, despite all the sign-posts and all the straws in the world's winds, that the day is gone when foreign relations are a "prerogative of the crown" or of a few leaders of the state.

This is said even though it should be recognized that there is a defense for a policy of at least semi-secrecy. Diplomacy is a touch-and-go business and one that cannot be conducted in a goldfish bowl or in a store window. Open diplomacy is a brave and resounding phrase, but in practice it is often far less effective than closed diplomacy. "Open covenants"—yes, but "openly arrived at"—very doubtful.[4]

---

[4] On this point there are these interesting observations by Paul-Henri Spaak, Prime Minister of Belgium ("The Role of the General Assembly," *International Conciliation,* November 1948) :

". . . we must consider whether we could not arrive at a somewhat more moderate system somewhere between secret diplomacy and open diplomacy as we are practicing it today.

"In order to explain and defend this idea, I have used a comparison drawn from cooking. I said, 'I understand quite well that we must describe the dish to the public, the menu that we want to have them eat, and I am ready to give them this menu with all the necessary details and descriptions. But is it absolutely necessary that the diplomatic cook should also explain and demonstrate in public how the dish is made?

"'I wish the public would stay in the dining-room and let us retire into the kitchen. They tell me that in the best restaurants one must think twice before going into the kitchen to see how the potatoes and vegetables are pared and the dishes washed. There are always things that it would be better not to see.

"'Well, diplomacy seems to me a little bit like cooking. The menu is for you. You have the right and we are in duty bound to an explanation of what we are trying to do and what aims we have set ourselves. But if you let us do the cooking in our own way, and let us do it quietly, perhaps we shall achieve better results.'"

A diplomat is a combination of statesman and poker player. Moreover, he must pay a good deal of attention to "face"—his own and his nation's—and make every effort to preserve both. Too often, if a position is taken openly, the diplomat feels he must stand by it uncompromisingly, for the sake of face. Whereas, if a position is taken behind closed doors and therefore tentatively, some compromise is possible. And inasmuch as in this uncertain and imperfect world the ideal solution is not easily found, compromise is often the half loaf that is better than none.

It is argued also that men entrusted with vast policy questions should act according to their best judgments, without regard to the popular view. Walter Lippmann puts the case this way:

> He [Monroe] did what he conceived to be right and necessary. The correspondence of the three Virginia Presidents is concerned not with what the Gallup Poll might show about the opinions of the people, but with what the vital interests of the country required in the situation as it presented itself.[5]

These arguments have much validity, but, at the same time, account must be taken of the importance of the public opinion factor in foreign policy. That factor cannot be ignored, the need of secrecy, the unhindered judgment and the dilemma notwithstanding. This applies to all branches of the government. For example, there is the prime question of what our policy shall be with regard to information about the atom bomb. There has been, on the part of the White House and the Atomic Energy Commission, a tendency to hold to a policy of strictest secrecy. That policy is questioned by Bradley Dewey in these words:

> We need a high policy governing our employment of atomic weapons in war. The American people must participate in this policy, must accept it and be willing to support it. To do this they

---

[5] Walter Lippmann, *U. S. Foreign Policy: Shield of the Republic,* Boston, Little, Brown, 1943, p. 85.

must have facts which have been kept from them by the White House.[6]

The conduct of modern war requires the enrollment of every citizen in the military effort. The conduct of foreign policy, if it is to insure peace and prosperity, requires the same kind of free cooperation. In a dictatorship, there is the Word and then the March—fiats and frenzy are substituted for public opinion. In a democracy, there must be understanding and conviction; there will not be blind support of a policy proclaimed from above. That is why the nation requires frank treatment from its government. That is why the era of white-shuttered diplomacy must be declared officially ended.

3. The Hugeness of the Job

Frank treatment, yes; government must play its part. But the citizen must play his part also; he must recognize his responsibility and he must make a greater effort to equip himself for citizenship. Consider these findings:

Item: About three out of ten voters are unaware of almost every event in American foreign affairs.

Item: About sixty-five out of every 100 voters admit that they rarely discuss foreign affairs.

Item: Only twenty-five out of every 100 voters can be considered reasonably well informed, and even in this sector there are large areas of ignorance.

Item: One month before Congress authorized the Marshall Plan (after months of Congressional debate and public discussion), sixteen out of 100 voters had never heard of it; only fourteen out of 100 could give a reasonably correct statement of the Plan's purpose.

Item: Only sixteen out of 100 Americans can give a reasonable explanation of how the veto in the United Nations Security Council works.

[6] "High Policy and the Atomic Bomb," *Atlantic Monthly,* December 1948, p. 39.

Despite our participation in two world wars, despite our present gestures of help for Europe, despite the appearance we assume of having forever forsaken isolationism, there are many among us who are still at the core isolationist; who still distrust anything foreign; who are inclined to look upon Uncle Sam as a combination of Santa Claus and Lady Bountiful.

Thomas A. Bailey, in his study of attitudes of the average American, sums it up this way:

> . . . the Man in the Street is a rugged individualist who has learned to hoe his own row without foreign support, who has developed an inherent distrust of foreigners, who has no deep-seated interest in foreign trade, and who, with true Yankee thrift, does not like to squander his money fighting what he conceives to be "other people's wars." [7]

These facts indicate the proportions and the complexity of the task that confronts our government in winning the support of the nation even for a fairly simple foreign program—the barriers of ignorance and prejudice that must be overcome.[8]

If public opinion at home seems to call for a large educational effort to make our policies and our objectives clear, the same is true of the state of public opinion abroad with regard to us. Communists everywhere in Europe, on both sides of the Iron Curtain, picture the United States as a hotbed of reaction and capitalist exploitation. Even in democratic circles, the pre-war caricature of Americans persists —a portrait of a naive, aggressive and vulgar people. Throughout Western Europe, it is true, the United States is preferred to Soviet Russia, but the preference is negative, resting more on fear of Russian Communism than on admiration and respect for the American way of life.[9]

The visitor to Europe is astonished and dismayed by the

---

[7] *The Man in the Street,* New York, Macmillan, 1948, p. 245.
[8] These barriers are described more fully by Dr. Kriesberg in Chapter Two.
[9] These attitudes are analyzed by Mr. Stone in Chapter Seven.

depths of ignorance about us; by the height of the walls against us that have been built by piling prejudice on top of prejudice; by the singleness and ruthlessness of the totalitarian way arrayed against the more humane and softer approaches of democracy.

These conditions indicate the proportions of the propaganda task that confronts us in foreign lands. Too many of us believe we are so definitely right in our dealings with other nations, and believe it so self-righteously, that we see no need of defending or explaining ourselves. Obviously, we say, we are an honest, altruistic people. But a good part of the world does not believe these things; therefore, it is not pertinent to inquire whether foreigners are right or wrong in their disbeliefs about us; the one important consideration now is the fact itself: that they disbelieve.

* * *

There are then two massive tasks that confront us in the opinion field, one at home and one abroad. These are not separate operations; each is the natural and necessary complement of the other. In each we must learn to use public opinion both as *directive* and as *instrument.*

Public opinion, used as *directive,* provides guide-posts for our foreign policy, defining its limits, indicating what is possible and what impossible, and thus making more probable support at home and acceptance abroad.

Public opinion, used as *instrument,* provides the unity at home that is vital to any government program and the understanding abroad that is indispensable if we are to achieve our international objectives.

4. Some Propaganda for Propaganda

At this point, as we begin a survey of the large issues involved in these operations, we encounter two words: "propaganda" and "information." It is important that the two be defined at the outset.

Yes, let us discuss words, because unless we understand them they are likely to bedevil us and lead us into false paths. The world is in pressing need of a new international dictionary. Consider, for example, how contradictory are the definitions of the word "democracy." For the Russians it has one meaning—an economic interpretation, and it implies the acceptance of a police state. For us it has another meaning—we emphasize political rather than economic democracy, believing that unless you have the first you cannot have the second; and we stress individual freedom.

Or the words "left" and "right." Left and right of what? Was Hitler "right" and is Stalin "left"? Yet both believed in a kind of national socialism, both built police states, both insisted that they spoke for the people. Or words such as "patriotism" or "national interests" or "security" or "internationalism" or even "truth." The list can be extended indefinitely until the dictionary becomes a kind of Wonderland in which the chief figure is Humpty Dumpty who says, as he said to Alice: "When I use a word, it means just what I choose it to mean—neither more nor less."

Especially let us consider the word "propaganda." It evokes thunder and lightning—a blitz of emotion—among Americans anywhere, but especially in Washington and particularly on Capitol Hill. Whenever propagandists (or even members of that lesser tribe, publicity men) approach its corridors, Congress sounds the alarm.

All this is strange to contemplate in a nation which, more than any other in history, is addicted to advertising, which is a push-over for slogans and shibboleths. For what is advertising but propaganda intended to win friends and influence people to buy a particular product? What are the speeches made by Congressional denouncers of "propaganda" except propaganda for their own legislative remedies? Strange, indeed, this fear of a single word, but there it is.

The dread of the weighted word is so great that it is actually written into the laws. In 1913 the Department of Agriculture decided to employ a public relations man. The outcry in the Congress was huge and horrendous; here was an executive department actually proposing to set up machinery that, by operating on the minds of voters, might bring pressure to bear on recalcitrant Congressmen.

Now, perhaps, too many kind words should not be said about public relations men in government. But the threat of one appointment seems hardly serious enough to warrant an act of Congress making unlawful the use of federal funds "for the compensation of any publicity expert unless specifically appropriated for that purpose." [10]

Be that as it may, the law was duly passed and is on the books today. If it were rigidly applied, it would make illegal almost any press release regarding almost any matter before Congress, because a simple communiqué—far more innocent than many a speech made in Congress—might set in motion a chain reaction in public opinion which would have its effect, directly or indirectly, on legislation. For example, if Secretary Marshall, after the introduction of the ERP legislation in Congress, had distributed a statement expressing himself in favor of the legislation, his action could easily have been construed, under the 1913 statute, as a criminal act.

There have been no prosecutions under this law, but it is not one of those that are filed away and forgotten. Its existence is kept constantly in mind by officials in the executive branch charged with maintaining relations with the press and the public, and it acts as an omnipresent check upon them. That fear inhibits executive departments from asking for funds that are necessary if the information job is to be done properly; it prevents the procurement of outstanding

---

[10] *United States Code,* 1913, title 5, sec. 54. Six years later further legislation prohibited the use of federal funds, unless expressly authorized by Congress, to pay for "publicity" intended to influence a member of Congress with respect to legislation. (*United States Code,* 1919, title 18, sec. 201.)

experts for government public opinion work; in brief, it cripples any real propaganda program.

In office after office in Washington, you discuss what needs to be done in the way of informing and educating public opinion. The officials with whom you talk agree fully, and then they look around their rooms and say in hushed voices, "But we shall be accused of propaganda," and they shrink into silence.

You wonder whether there is any foundation for so fearsome a fear of a single word. And so you turn, for a possible clue, to the history of "propaganda."

5. *What Is "Propaganda"?*

The word is derived from the Latin *propagare*—"to extend, enlarge, increase, carry forward, advance, spread." It came into general usage (though not at all in the present sense) in the seventeenth century, after the creation in 1622 by Pope Gregory XV of the *Sacra Congregatio de Propaganda Fide*—the Sacred Congregation for the Propagation of the Faith, which became known later simply as "The Propaganda." The Propaganda has been since then, and still is, one of the most important of the Roman congregations; it is charged with the administration of all church affairs in non-Catholic countries and one of its primary functions is the supervision of all foreign missions. The use of the word "propaganda" by the Church had none of the unsavory implications which attach to it today. The activity described was no different from that contemplated by Jesus when He admonished His disciples: "Go ye into all the world and preach the Gospel to every creature."

In the political as well as the religious field—up to the time of the satanic propagandists of the twentieth century—the word had no inherently evil connotation. The orations of Pericles and Cicero were indubitably propaganda and were recognized as such; the torch-bearers of the French Revolution, such men as Voltaire and Rousseau, and of the

American Revolution, men like Paine and Jefferson, were, in the same sense, propagandists. Wilson's Fourteen Points were surely propaganda, put out to further the cause of democracy. And so the examples out of history could be cited indefinitely.

With the development of total warfare in the first World War and the consequent attention directed by governments to influencing the attitudes of great masses of people, the uses of propaganda were widely extended. "By degrees, the conquest of neutral opinion was seen to be almost as important as victory in the field." [11]

In the period between the World Wars, the instruments of communication (the tools of propaganda) were developed to an extraordinary degree. The radio, especially, became a new and gigantic factor in moulding public opinion. In the Russian revolution Lenin and his followers used propaganda more expertly than it had ever been used before. Then, with the coming of Hitler and the incredible Goebbels, the propaganda tool acquired its sharpest edge.

"We have made the Reich by propaganda," said Goebbels in 1939—and, for once, he was not lying. There is no doubt that the rise of the Nazi party was due in considerable degree to the manipulation of opinion in Germany. Goebbels, with his blazing words and his blaring loudspeakers, kept together for years what was thought at the time to be a great monolithic column, but which is now revealed to have been a structure as full of cracks as is Hitler's great amphitheater in Nuremberg today.

The frightfulness of those days is still burnt into our memory—the vast assemblies, with their serried, hook-crossed ranks; the thunderous, grating utterances of the Fuehrer; the unrelenting assault on the emotions, like that of an African chief beating out his call to war. Back of it all was falsehood. "By clever, persistent propaganda even

---

[11] From the excellent article on the subject in the *Encyclopaedia Britannica*, v. 18, p. 582.

Heaven can be represented to a people as Hell and the most wretched life as Paradise," says Hitler in *Mein Kampf.* And again: "A definite factor in getting a lie believed is the size of the lie. The broad mass of the people, in the simplicity of their hearts, more easily fall victim to a big lie than a small one."

Thus, because the Word was a lie, propaganda came to be known as an evil thing. And the blackness of the connotation deepened when we fell out with the Russians after the war and they began to use propaganda as a major weapon in the contest of nerves and ideas.

But it is important to look at this history without emotion so that we shall judge it for what it is. If we do, we conclude that what is to be deplored is not the instrument itself but the evil use of it; that propaganda in itself is neither good nor bad, it is a method, a technique. If it is employed skillfully and for good ends, it has its great uses for us, too.

6. *On the Other Hand—Information*

Against the word "propaganda" there is often put the word "information," as if it were the direct opposite. The difference is not always clear-cut and simple; it might be put, broadly, this way:

Information is the communication of facts and opinions in an effort to enlighten.

Propaganda is the communication of facts (or non-facts) and opinions in an effort to influence.

Information, presumably, is calm, coldly logical, unemotional; propaganda is turbulent, hotly persuasive, supercharged with emotion. But the distinction is not that easy. On the one hand, propaganda may be the utterly calm presentation of lies. On the other hand, facts set down coolly and objectively often have a greater influence than flaming, unfactual words. Moreover, the selection of certain facts as against others may cause a greater reaction than the most resounding sequence of sentences.

Yet, even though at times the line between "propaganda" and "information" is only dimly seen, there is a basic difference—a difference that is especially important when we attempt to determine the approach and the method to be used in dealing with public opinion. In the light of the preceding discussion, our two tasks (in the areas of opinion at home and opinion abroad) might be defined in this way:

1.) The domestic task is basically to give the American people the facts and reasons behind our foreign policy so that they will understand it and, presumably, support it. This, because it is an effort to enlighten, is an *information* job.

2.) The foreign task is basically to make certain that we are understood by other peoples, that our purposes and programs are clearly set out so that our own cause may be furthered abroad. This, because it is an attempt to convince, is a *propaganda* job.[12]

While similar forces play upon opinion both here and abroad, while human emotions are the same and reactions tend to be alike the world over, nevertheless there are differences in political forms, in national traditions and especially in economic conditions that make the two tasks in many respects dissimilar.

At home our democratic system assumes that government policies reflect the desires of the people. If enlightened public opinion is opposed to a policy, it is taken for granted that there will be an effort to make the policy conform, not the opinion. On the other hand, the fact that an American policy may be unpopular abroad is not necessarily a reason for abandoning, or even modifying, that policy. Certainly many of our policies have been distasteful to the Communist

[12] A fuller discussion of the objectives in the State Department's foreign operations will be found in Chapter Eight.

and Fascist governments and will prove so in the future; we cannot be expected to alter them to remove that displeasure. Our task in these instances is to try, through propaganda, to convince the people in Communist and Fascist areas that our course is correct, in spite of all their leaders may say in derogation of it.

Despite these differences between information and propaganda, it should be recognized that the two are parts of a whole. They are not separate tools, but two edges of the one instrument. Truth is the essence of information. It must be the essence of propaganda, also, if propaganda is to prevail. A Goebbels may have a temporary success, but sooner or later an edifice built on lies will crumble.

* * *

We have spent a good deal of time and space on definitions, but it is vital that we have our terms straight if we are to avoid detours and difficulties. Unless we do, we cannot bring proper understanding and perspective to our main undertaking—the analysis of the tasks at home and abroad.

7. Opinion at Home—Who Makes It?

Public opinion at home requires detailed study because it is—or it should be—one of the major keys to our foreign policy and because it determines, to considerable degree, our actions with regard to public opinion abroad.

What are the influences that mould our public opinion? How does that opinion manifest itself? What trends does it reveal?

Let us start, as we must, at the beginning—with the Average Man, that mythical creature who is always below or above average and yet is indispensable to us, psychologically as well as statistically.

The public (which is the average man in the aggregate) acquires the information—or the viewpoint—by which he arrives at an opinion either by eye or by ear. In the days before the radio it was the eye rather than the ear that was the important organ in the process; the printed word took decided precedence over the spoken word.

The printed word still retains its potency; there is a finality about anything graven, an authority that no spoken word can convey. Yet type is likely to be cold and unemotional, whereas the voice can be very warm and very persuasive. The radio reaches into the home with an intimacy of which print is incapable. Certainly no thunderer of old, neither Greeley nor Dana, had the mass power now available to a radio crusader. Thus today we must take full account of the appeal of the voice as well as the appeal of the printed word.

There are three great moulders of public opinion—the *government,* the *press* and the *citizen groups.*

The *government* exerts its influence on the public directly through official addresses and indirectly through contact with the press or private groups.

The *press* (the word is used here in its broadest sense, as in the Hutchins report,[13] to include all the media of mass communication) exerts its influence directly upon the public through 11,500 American newspapers (daily and weekly), 2,660 radio stations, the 1,000 pictures Hollywood produces each year, and the numberless publications put out by the magazine and book publishers.

The *citizen groups*—public forums, women's clubs, study groups of various kinds—are increasing in number. They are now estimated to number hundreds of thousands and they are playing an increasingly important role in the formation of public opinion.[14]

---

[13] Report by the Commission on Freedom of the Press, *A Free and Responsible Press,* Chicago, University of Chicago Press, 1947. Here the press is defined as "the major agencies of mass communication: radio, newspapers, motion pictures, magazines, and books."

[14] The number of clubs in the United States is indicated by the following figures: The American Legion has 16,802 posts; Rotary 3,692 clubs, Kiwanis 2,592 clubs and the Lions 5,750 clubs; affiliates of the General Federation of

In assessing debits and credits for the state of public opinion, obviously the performance of the press must be considered first; in most periods it is the outstanding factor in the moulding of opinion. There are years when a Roosevelt or a Churchill will make his voice heard above all others; at such times the press is likely to be only a chorus, either of assent or dissent. But this occurs only when two factors coincide: a personality of rare appeal and a period of grave emergency.

At other times, when one or the other of these factors is absent, the press has great power, either because of achievement in providing information and opinion or because of failure in neglecting to supply proper information or in furnishing misinformation and so inciting prejudice. Day-by-day access to the public, the massive and unceasing roar of the printing machines, the steady riveting of repetition, make the press, at most times, the most potent of the opinion forces.

The press has its shortcomings and they should be recognized. We have in the United States a free press, but we have yet to develop a fully responsible one. As for the newspapers, too many of them are preoccupied with comics, circulation capers and other business office devices, without full regard to the basic reason for their being—namely, as disseminators of the news. And much of the radio can be indicted on the same count of commercialism.

This problem of the function and responsibility of the American press is having, as it should have, increasing attention. The sanctity of the *sancta sanctorum* is being questioned.[15] Yet the remedy for the defects of any of the mass

---

Women's Clubs, 14,045. In addition, virtually every church, most high schools and all colleges have organizations devoted to current events or foreign affairs subjects. There are also innumerable independent clubs, both women's and men's, around the country.

[15] For example, in the debate over the Hutchins Report and the Nieman Fellows Report (An Account of an Educational Experiment Now in Its Tenth Year. Edited by Louis M. Lyons, Harvard University Press, October 1948).

media cannot be imposed from above, by government or otherwise, either through directive or censorship; it must come from the reader and the listener, who should demand better newspapers, better radio, better words in all media and on all subjects.

The citizen groups are far from being as effective as they might be in the formation of public opinion. Under their present organization and procedure these groups are likely to reach only persons who have already been exposed to information or who—and there are too many of these—are already converted to a point of view. The much larger groups in the dark areas of ignorance and misinformation must be reached. Citizen groups also show a tendency to go off at tangents because they do not realize fully what are the basic issues or the main points in controversy. They require, in other words, a larger dose of briefing—which is an assignment for both government and press.

But neither the performance of the press nor of the private groups is the proper concern of this study.[16] These are problems of the extension of adult education, the theme of another and much longer book than this. We are dealing here with the part played by government—by making, and making known, its foreign policy—in the moulding of public opinion. With regard to the press and the private groups, the only question here is whether the government does an effective job in informing them so that they, in turn, can properly inform their readers or listeners.

8. *Notes on the Policy Makers*

Let us turn now to the government agencies which deal with these public opinion problems. Let us consider policy and the policy makers.

When we talk about policy we are again likely, unless we are wary, to be bewitched by words. Policy seems to mean

[16] The discussion of the work of American private agencies abroad in Chapter Nine constitutes a special case.

something planned, definite, clean-cut—something that has come, shaped and firm, out of the ovens of debate. Yet it is not so, even in countries like Russia, where the ovens are rigidly controlled and the product searchingly scrutinized.

Washington is an amorphous place, made up of many men, many minds, many motives. Policy is likewise amorphous, and foreign policy especially, being an amalgam of politics, psychology and poker, cannot be exact—nor should it be, in a world as shifting and uncertain as the present one. Obviously we must move according to a chart of broad principles, but there must be an element of flexibility and even of opportunism in any foreign policy, especially in a world in which Russia, so opportunist herself, plays so large a part. Moreover, while the general strategy of our foreign policy is determined and the tactics outlined by the top brass the execution is left to the lesser metal. It sometimes happens, therefore, that the direction is set irrevocably by a minor official, making what is regarded at the time as a minor decision.[17]

Furthermore, in a democracy where, despite all the efficiency experts, reorganizations and charts, power is still divided among many branches and agencies of government and where decentralization still prevails, policy is made in various places—and often it is not coordinated.

For these reasons, the visitor to Washington, seeking to discover what our foreign policy is, will, in all likelihood, emerge confused and condemnatory. He will find that only dim outlines of policy can be recognized; in fact, that often there is no policy but only policies.

Foreign policy, or foreign policies, are made for the most part by four branches of the government—the *President,*

[17] For example, in American-occupied Germany following the Potsdam Agreement. The broad statement of policy in this agreement left so much room for varying interpretation that the American position on many questions had to be worked out by subordinate United States officials in Berlin, who were in only tenuous touch with Washington. Yet once a position had been taken and communicated to representatives of the other occupying powers in Germany, it became very difficult to alter.

the *Congress,* the *State Department* and the *Military.* Inasmuch as all policies depend, for their ultimate effectiveness, upon the support of public opinion, each agency must devote a good deal of attention to analyzing and informing that opinion.

The *President* makes public opinion constantly: in an address to Congress; in a chat—fireside or otherwise—to the nation; at a press conference in answer to questions inspired (as Roosevelt's often were inspired) by the Press Secretary, or non-inspired, as many are, from the newspaper critics of the Administration, and in other similar ways.

The real Voice of America in the United States is the voice of the President; he is expected to lead the way and set the tone; he is the commander of the task force assigned to implementing a foreign affairs program. If the President is able to do an effective radio job, he can win great support; in the case of a Roosevelt, he may almost hypnotize. Such a situation may have its dangers,[18] but the fact remains that the Number One Voice is the voice that spreads out over the land from the microphone in the Oval Room in the White House.

Congressmen influence public opinion through speeches, through direct contact with their constituents, through committee hearings and other public appearances.

The influence of the Congress in foreign policy is greater than ever before. In some ways the House is now as responsible for such policy as the Senate, even though the treaty-making power still resides in the Senate. Foreign policy in these days of economic stress is made through appropriations—and appropriations require the consent of the House. The Marshall Plan, for example, the very crux of our foreign policy today, is a money-spending policy; hence, its fate depends to considerable degree upon the Chairman of the House Appropriations Committee.

The Senate, possibly because of the recent invasion of the

---

[18] As Mr. Reston points out in Chapter Three.

House into a field which it considered its special and sacred preserve, is more insistent than ever before in asserting its surveillance over foreign affairs. And the so-called bipartisan policy brought about an unparalleled relationship in the field of foreign affairs between the Senate and the Executive.[19]

Because of the importance of Congess in the public opinion picture, the relations between Congress and the State Department should be close and good. They are neither. There is a great uncertainty about State on Capitol Hill; the average Congressman is apt to look upon the fellows in State as "cookie pushers" or "ivory tower boys." One is almost convinced that some Congressmen are suspicious of State Department officials because they are able to speak foreign languages—which makes them in a sense foreigners, and hence untrustworthy. Certainly there is something about the manner of the garden-party variety of diplomat that baffles and bothers the average M.C. These are creatures out of another world; certainly they are not "folks," not the kind of people he knows back home.

This distrust is evident in the grilling to which most members of the Department are subjected when they appear before Congressional committees. The investigations of the Department's activities in the information field seem almost endless; it has been estimated, for example, that in a six-month period in 1947 more that 1,000 man-days were devoted by State Department officials to describing and defending its opinion operations before various Congressional committees.

Many Congressmen seem to reason thus: if the executive agencies are permitted to try to influence public opinion, they may end up by controlling the public viewpoint so thoroughly that Congress will become a mere rubber stamp. To the unemotional observer these fears seem largely groundless. Safeguards already exist to insure that the Congress

---

[19] For a fuller discussion of these points see Chapter Four.

will not be dominated by government publicity agents. Also, Congress is accustomed to pressures. It seems strange that a body, which has dealt so long and so intensively with lobbies of all varieties, should fear lobbying by government agencies who can offer only the beguilement of words, not even the mild briberies of cocktail parties.

As for possible influence of executive departments on the public mind, we have to take our chances on that. If the facts swerve opinion, then Congress cannot object. The only concern Congress can legitimately have is that the publications of the government departments for circulation within the country shall be information, that is, factual presentation, rather than propaganda. Provided these safeguards are maintained, there seems little danger that the improvement of our information services will weaken in any way our system of government or the foundations of our democracy.

Congress is ultimately responsive to the point of view of the people, but it tends to lag behind the country. Its first reaction is timidity, fear that it will be putting its neck out or getting too far out on a limb. Congressmen, one is led to conclude, mend their fences not to keep their constituents properly corralled within them but rather to be able to sit comfortably upon them. That is why public opinion, to impress the Congress, needs to be both well informed and definitely assertive.

The *Military* is the third agency that makes American opinion in the field of foreign policy—through releases, through propaganda for various projects in which it is especially interested, such as universal military training, through the speeches of generals and admirals, and through the impact of the Department of Defense on other departments. The Defense Department can strongly influence policy. For example, it is customary for the Secretary of Defense to point out the danger spots in the world that have been revealed to him through his intelligence division. He does that, you are told, in order that the Department of Defense shall be prepared to meet the problems for which it is responsible. Yet, by informing the State Department that a dangerous situation exists in a certain part of the world and inquiring what the State Department policy is, the Defense Department virtually selects the areas on which attention is to be focused.

Discussion of the Defense Department leads inevitably to a survey of the Military Mind. That is a subject for long and deep debate,[20] but for the immediate purposes it is sufficient only to consider its tendency toward narrowness of outlook—which is not surprising since obedience and singleness of purpose are the two chief marks of the military.

The narrow view helps to explain why differences often arise between the military and political divisions of the Government. The first looks at any problem primarily from the viewpoint of defense while the second will also take into account the political and psychological implications. Consider, for example, the argument over whether we should adopt a more lenient attitude toward the Franco régime in Spain. The Military tended at times to favor a softer policy toward Franco because they were thinking about air bases in Spain in the event of war with Russia. The State Department, on the other hand, has been opposed on the ground that a good part of Europe would be shocked by what to them would be appeasement of a dictator. In this broader view, military advantage would be far outweighed by political disadvantage.

The fourth agency that contributes, either by thought or action, to foreign policy is, of course, the *Department of State*. Because it is the Department that maintains constant liaison with other nations, because this is our Foreign Ministry, because this is the Department closest to the White

---

[20] Mr. Baldwin, who knows that mind through observation both in and outside the services, offers some illuminating remarks in this connection in Chapter Five.

House, the State Department has, as it should have, the ranking place in this book.[21]

9. *Quick Portrait of the State Department*

The loci and nature of the State Department operations are many, and often more than passing strange. It functions in a streamlined army building in Washington, in a converted apartment house in the capital, in an office building in New York, in mansions in London, Paris and Buenos Aires, in a requisitioned private home in Berlin, in a hut in Africa. In a single day State Department officials will be making speeches in Bogotá and in fifty other places; they will be conferring on open covenants, unopenly arrived at, in the blue and mahogany rooms of the Washington headquarters; they will be broadcasting from a station in New York; they will be trying to gauge opinion in the United States; they will be calling upon presidents and kings and labor leaders abroad; they will be gathering information in all quarters of the world.

The officials are almost as diverse as the operations. In the main they fall into two great divisions: the Career Men and the Circumstance Men. The former, who in many cases have been attracted to the State Department because of its prestige and its traditions, are likely to look upon themselves as an upper caste; the latter, who have joined the Department in most instances because they were seeking to make a living in the public service, constitute another caste —not necessarily higher or lower, but surely distinct.

The Department is divided, broadly, between the geographical desks and the information desks.

To the geographical desks come the reports from our

---

[21] One gauge of the increasing importance of the State Department and its expanding functions is the growth of personnel. Here are the figures (including the Foreign Service):

1790—25	1913—1,836	1943— 7,625
1833—206	1922—3,920	1948—16,139
1870—850	1938—4,652	1949—16,443

diplomatic representatives abroad, and from them come recommendations for action by the Secretary and Under-Secretary. In the main they comprise the *Policy-Making Group;* often by their decisions in lesser matters, or by their detailed interpretations of broad programs, they set the line of policy so firmly that it is difficult to shift.

The information desks are concerned with the dissemination and the explanation of policy. Theirs is a much less cosmic and frock-coated function. No ambassadors or even chargés d'affaires call at their offices to discuss deep questions of state; to them protocol is only a word in the dictionary of diplomacy. They belong, for the most part, to the *Policy-Promoting Group.*

The geographical desks are likely to be manned by Career Men; the information desks by Circumstance Men. The two groups, as has been indicated, are of two different strata; they do not mingle, especially at social functions. This social cleavage helps to explain failures to integrate policy. Because foreign policy is a nebulous thing, as much psychology as politics, State Department business is as likely to be conducted at social gatherings—luncheons, dinners and, of course, cocktail parties, at which both members of the Department and foreign diplomats often are present—as in the official chambers on Twenty-first Street, N.W. Thus the two groups do not meet at what are sometimes the most important of the meeting places.

The Career Men, in many cases nurtured and reared behind the white shutters, are less likely than the Circumstance Men to be in contact with the Average Man and hence less aware of the importance of public opinion.

This kind of blind spot is by no means confined to the Career Men in the Department. Even among expert groups studying the organization of the State Department, public opinion activities are likely to be considered a side issue in its work, or as footnotes to its programs. That is a false and dangerous misconception.

Public opinion, whether it be controlled, as in Russia, or uncontrolled, as in the United States, plays so important a role in foreign policy that it must be treated as a matter of the first importance. The public opinion operation in the State Department should be accorded full status for two reasons:

First, appraisal of public opinion is essential to the formulation of foreign policy. Certainly it would be unwise to adopt any program if it were clear either that the country would not support it or that our friends abroad would find it distasteful. This is *the intelligence function* of the Department.

Second, cultivation of public opinion is vital to the execution of any foreign policy. Unless the support of the American people, and of nations associated with us abroad, can be obtained for the program, it will surely fail in the long run. This is *the information (and propaganda) function* of the Department.

With these basic elements in mind, let us consider how the two functions—intelligence and information-propaganda—are carried out by the Department, first at home and then abroad.

10. *State Department and Opinion at Home*

The set-up in the State Department for dealing with public opinion is a highly complex one.[22] If, as many critics contend, it does not function as well as it should, the reasons will be found primarily in the fact that opinion has not been recognized as a vital element in foreign policy, and, secondarily, in certain defects in organization and execution. An examination of the performance in the domestic area reveals some of these weaknesses.

The *intelligence function* is primarily the assignment of the Public Studies Division. Each day the Division supplies to leading members of the Department a mimeographed

[22] For the detailed picture see the charts on pp. 122, 160.

sheet, marked "restricted," in which the public opinion of the day is digested. It is an attempt to round up national opinion for the guidance of the Department—a compilation of editorial articles, of statements by the nation's leaders, a summary of the polls.

Despite the difficulties of the assignment and the shortage of staff,[23] the intelligence operation has a definite value. While editorial and other so-called top opinion in the country does not represent general opinion it does give important clues as to what the leaders of opinion are thinking.

The polls deserve special attention. Until the Presidential election of 1948, considerable weight was attached to these surveys. They had been a basic pigment in the political picture; many politicians were awed by this kind of mathematics. It remains to be seen what will be the effects of the revelation of their weaknesses.

This observer has always been skeptical of the polls. It is possible that the pollster may be able to work out a system of forecasting an election "scientifically" and accurately. That possibility seems extremely remote, but concede, for the sake of argument, that it can be done. Even then two vital questions remain: First, what value have such forecasts? Second, what about the other and more important samplings?

As for the value in the case of elections, there is none, as the pollster himself will admit. If there were any, why should we not dispense with the election itself and so save ourselves a tidy sum? On the other hand, the polls may work positive harm in bringing about an apathy in the electorate or in stimulating a band-wagon vote.

The second question is the much more important one. It had been assumed, because the polls had, until the last election, forecast the electoral vote fairly accurately, that their findings on national issues (for example, on aid to Europe) were also of great value. But that assumption is now open

[23] See Chapter Six for a fuller discussion of this point.

to grave doubt. In polls on national issues the ballots taken are far fewer in number than in forecasting elections.[24] Would one be cynical if one asked whether this is because there is no way of checking the accuracy of a poll not followed by an election?

There are other defects: the polls on national issues take for granted a background of knowledge that simply does not exist; there is no recognition of the prestige factor—few people will admit ignorance even to a reassuring pollster; and there is no weighing of intensity of feeling about an issue.

The poll, then, fortunately, has been dethroned from its high place. Government, Congress and the people will be better off. Yet it must be recognized that polls have had and still have a certain value in the study of public opinion. Ironically, they have proved useful in a way for which they were not intended, viz., to indicate what people do not know. To locate the areas of ignorance is important for the questions with which we are dealing here.

In addition to the polls, there are the compilations that the Division of Public Studies makes of what editors, columnists and commentators are saying about foreign policy. These, too, require careful analysis because the drawing of any large deductions from this kind of data is a delicate undertaking.

In connection with the Division's daily public opinion digests, various questions arise: Are the compilations properly studied and summarized so as to be useful to policy makers? And even if the Division's reports were greatly improved, this question remains: will they obtain either the perusal or the attention they deserve? This question is not rhetorical. A high officer of the Department and a wise observer of men and events has said: "We read the digests, we ponder the polls, and then we are likely to be influenced by our favorite columnist."

[24] In elections it is something around 60,000; on national issues it is 3,000.

On two scores then—first, in improvement of the reports and second, in the uses to which they are put—changes are needed if the Department is to carry out effectively its first assignment in the opinion job at home—*the intelligence function*.

As for the second assignment—the *information function*—there are two directions in which the Department carries on its domestic operation. First, there is the direct appeal to the public through speeches and statements by members of the Department and through the pamphlets and other materials made available by its Office of Public Affairs. Second, there is the press, to which material is funneled for dissemination to the public.

The effectiveness of the speeches by the Secretary, the Under-Secretary and other members of the Department depends, as does all oratory, on the integrity and the sincerity of the speaker and of his speech. Too many addresses made in Washington are prepared by ghost writers and the product is often as pallid and as elusive as a ghost itself. Timidity and artificiality intrude too much into such productions. Yet when an official of character and force will speak in his own way, setting out his own thoughts with an honesty that often horrifies the ghosts, he is likely to win the confidence of his hearers to a degree that no synthetic oration can ever achieve.

The operations of the Office of Public Affairs have become increasingly important. By supplying informational material to writers and speakers, by suggestions to clubs for programs, by the publication of "background" pamphlets for the general public, the Office provides basic material for national discussion. This is an essential service, yet it cannot equal in importance the direct approach to the public through speeches by Department members and statements issued through the press.

The Department's relations with the press deserve special scrutiny. These are days when the news is complex and most difficult to grasp. It is one world from the informational as well as the geographic point of view. Politics cannot be divorced from economics, nor from psychology; a new equation in science may change the whole international situation; a new method of communication may alter the temper of public opinion the world over. Therefore—notably in the misty areas of foreign policy—it is not enough for the government to give the press mere facts. There is more to be read between the lines than on them.

To the facts must be added interpretation—by which is meant not opinion about the facts or the passing of judgment upon them, but a statement of their meaning, their significance. The press has not assumed the task of interpretation to the degree that is essential. It must do more if we are to have the kind of public opinion we need. But the press must have help from government in that endeavor. The State Department cannot consider its job done if it merely issues factual statements, especially because most official communiqués are intended to conceal rather than reveal. The Department must be prepared to explain to the press why an action is taken, and what are the implications. It must set up the machinery necessary for such briefing of the press.[25]

This is said with full realization of the difficulty of the briefing task. Here again it should be pointed out that while open diplomacy is a brave and wonderful ideal, it cannot be practiced to its last implication. Yet the doors need not be as tightly closed as they are now; they should not be, for the good of the Department as well as of the country.

11. *The Challenge of Communism*

In Moscow, the radio blares to all Europe that the Marshall Plan is a device to enchain the continent; in Bucharest, in a building whose innocent look is belied by the blacked-

---

[25] Mr. Davison has described (in Chapter Six, pp. 136-39) the kind of change in the present machinery that might do the job.

out windows of the lower floors, the Cominform has set up G. H. Q. for political and propaganda activities throughout Europe; in Southern Italy the peasant reads only what the Communist paper tells him, no voice of America reaches him; in France *L'Humanité* spreads the party line to thousands of comrades who believe only what they want to believe. And so it goes in a good part of Europe, which is being told, day after day, by radio and by direct approach, that we are intent on capturing the world for our brand of capitalism, that our motives are purely selfish, that there is light only in the Kremlin.[26]

The Communists are adept and skillful propagandists. Their occasional blunders are due doubtless to the Marxian blind spots which make them refuse to accept reality when it does not agree with theory. On the whole, though, their successes considerably outnumber their failures. They go at the war of words with unrelenting energy and grant no quarter. They do not hesitate to throw all the adjectives and the book itself at their opponents. Their appeal is direct, unceasing and unscrupulous.

The Communists do not attempt precision bombing in their propaganda warfare; they spray whole areas, concentrating much of their fire on the lower income levels, where conditions are worst and education least. Communist emissaries work from house to house, shifting their arguments as a local situation may warrant, without any reverence whatsoever for consistency. They make speeches in parliaments and on street corners; they strive to gain influence by persuasion and often by terror.

The Communists depend heavily on their newspapers to put across the Communist credos. In a way these newspapers constitute their most effective weapon; in many areas of Europe they are the only news publications which reach large parts of the public. The news they publish is about as objec-

---

[26] The Communist method is described more fully by Mr. Stone in Chapter Seven.

tive as a speech by Stalin himself, but it must be kept in mind that foreign newspapers and foreign newspaper readers are not as concerned as Americans are (or should be) with the objectivity of the news. What the worker abroad is likely to get, therefore, is news with a slant.

It is true that all the Communist propaganda would be worthless unless there were a fertile field for it in the distressing economic state of Europe. It is true also that the ultimate cure is the application of economic remedies; that containment of Russian communism can be achieved only through amelioration of the lot of the common man. But it becomes more obvious daily that without political and psychological reinforcement, economic measures will fail, for lack of the spiritual nourishment that understanding supplies. This is the way the task is described by the Smith-Mundt report:

> It is the responsibility of the United States to affirm without reserve the ideas and ideals which motivate our course of action in the world. . . . But with all the good will in the world, the United States, unless trusted by the ordinary people of Europe, cannot help them in their perplexity. They must first know and understand us, then they will believe us.
> . . . Communist propaganda is busily engaged in distorting and maligning American life and motives. This effort is rendered all the easier by the false picture already existing in the mind of the average European. We must substitute knowledge and truth for ignorance and falsehood. Inasmuch as truth is our best weapon, we should not hesitate to make effective use of it.[27]

Thus the two insistent facts about public opinion in Europe are these: there is the Communist propaganda weapon and there are many targets at which it can be aimed. In recent months the cold war has broadened so that a good part of Asia is now included in the area of combat. There, too, the Communist propaganda machine is steadily at work and there, too, there are many foci of infection and distress

---

[27] Report of the Committee on Foreign Relations, No. 855, pursuant to S. Res. 161, 80th Congress, 2nd Session, 1948, pp. 3, 4. The Committee was composed of eighteen members of the Senate and House who went abroad in the Summer of 1947 to survey our information services.

in which the Communist agitator finds desperate response.

The challenge must be faced for what it is, an ideological struggle which must be fought with the instrument unhesitatingly called "propaganda." That effort requires a vigorous, combined operation of both government and private industry.

The propaganda map of the world can be divided into areas of three colors; in Europe, for example, it would look like this:

The black areas—the lands behind the Iron Curtain, into which outside thought penetrates only by accident, or by great ingenuity.

The white areas—the lands like England or the Benelux countries, which are free from thought control and where the Communist propaganda makes little dent.

The gray areas—the lands like Italy and France where the war of words is being hotly fought and where the shadow of the Kremlin always overhangs.[28]

The color of the area determines the nature of our propaganda operations, whether the major task shall be done by government or left to private enterprise, whether the emphasis shall be on long-term or short-term programs. (There are, it should be kept in mind, two kinds of information-propaganda programs. The long-range program is one based on cultural and educational elements; the short-term program is one based on discussion of immediate issues. In the first, time does not press; in the second, time presses hard and incessantly.)

In the *white areas,* the job is one primarily for private enterprise, with some cultural exchange under the auspices of the government. This is a long-term program. In the *black areas,* where private enterprise is barred, the assignment is clearly one for government. Here it is almost solely a short-term program; we are engaged in a continuous cam-

---

[28] Reports of the propaganda war as it is waged in Italy and France will be found in Chapter Ten.

paign to establish the truth. In the *gray areas* it is a joint operation, with private enterprise doing the work so far as it can and government filling in the gaps, which may be, as in the case of Italy, very large ones. At present, when the ideological struggle is so bitter, we are chiefly concerned with countering the day-by-day onslaughts of the Communists. Yet even here long-term as well as short-term programs are needed.

Let us consider now what is being done—and what needs to be done—in the opinion operation abroad, by the government and by the private agencies. Just as is the case in the domestic program, there are two facets in each of these foreign operations: *intelligence* and *information-propaganda*.

12. *The State Department and Opinion Abroad*

We cannot embark with assurance upon any political or propaganda program abroad unless we have ample and accurate information about the attitudes of the people whom we are trying to influence. Yet our *intelligence* reports on foreign public opinion at the present time are very scanty and very casual. Especially is this true in the areas behind the Iron Curtain. We make a Russian policy, but our information about Russia is very slight indeed.

For gauging foreign opinion—a job of reporting that is infinitely more complex than the domestic job—the Department must rely on its representatives abroad. The officials to whom this intelligence task is assigned can give only part time to it and are generally overworked. Yet, even if they had the time it is doubtful whether they could procure the kind of information that is needed. In the first place, they have had no training in the techniques of opinion analysis, and, in the second place, our diplomatic representatives abroad are career men; that means too often that they are not sufficiently in touch with the people in the countries where they are stationed, but rely, instead, on what they are told officially in foreign offices or unofficially at social functions. Finally, there is a tendency among officials in Washington to rate their own deductions over the reports that come from the field; there have been not infrequent complaints from envoys that their communiqués do not have the careful scrutiny which they think they deserve. All this indicates that an intelligence service is needed abroad which will be at least as effective as the set-up in Washington assigned to gauge domestic public opinion.

In its *information-propaganda* operation abroad the government uses both long-term and short-term instrumentalities. For the longer period it employs, in the main, information agencies; for the shorter period, under the pressure of time, it employs propaganda tools.

The long-term instruments include libraries of information, exchange of editors, of professors and of students, pamphlets and other documentary materials, cultural approaches of all kinds. The impact of these on opinion is slow, but it can be very sure.

Of the short-term instruments, the Voice of America has received the most attention. Up to two years ago there was an inclination in this country to consider the Voice an impractical experiment. But, with the increasing pressure from the Kremlin, and with the greater appreciation of the psychological war acquired by the numerous members of the House and Senate who have gone abroad, it has gained much wider understanding and support.[29]

The effectiveness of the Voice of America is still a matter of heated discussion. On the one hand there is the kind of attack that comes from John O'Donnell[30]: "The record shows that some of the 'good-will' foreign language broadcasts sent out by the staff of 184 individuals in the State Department's Division of International Broadcasting—where some twenty draw fat top-bracket paychecks and swank

---

[29] Largely as a result of the Mundt-Nixon report the Eightieth Congress increased the appropriations for the Information Services from $17,000,000 in the fiscal year of 1948 to $28,000,000 in 1949.

[30] That caustic columnist of the McCormick-Patterson chain.

around with hoity toity titles—are a matter for hilarious guffaws at our expense." O'Donnell talks often and freely of the "Voice of America screwballs" and the "balderdash the Voice of America is churning up."

On the other hand, you get from the Smith-Mundt Committee the statement that the Voice has an important function to perform. The committee puts it this way: "Since radio can be made the principal medium for reaching the masses in 'behind the curtain' countries, a careful study should be made as to the most efficient and effective means of making the fullest use of both the Voice of America and local broadcasting stations in Europe." [31]

That the Voice of America has value is without dispute. Its value would have been greater if Congress had not been reluctant to appropriate large sums for what it considered essentially a "propaganda" operation. Also, its effectiveness has been curtailed by the lack of a clear-cut policy in the Department regarding its use. At times, those engaged in the operation have been hard pressed to discover exactly what American policy was in a particular case.

Finally, there is no doubt that the Voice operation has not been handled as efficiently or as astutely as it might have been. Whether because of the failure of Congress to allot enough money to do the job competently, or because of amateur management, there have been errors of a high order. Some of these were made by the broadcasting companies, to whom a major part of the operation was at one time farmed out, but certainly the directors of the Voice could have been expected to exercise closer supervision.[32]

[31] Report of the Committee on Foreign Relations, *op. cit.,* p. 10.
[32] That basic defect in the Voice operation has been corrected. As a gesture toward free enterprise some 75 percent of the broadcasting was originally contracted to the National and Columbia broadcasting companies, which prepared the scripts under the general (and loose) supervision of the State Department. Thus the bulk of the operation was, in effect, not the Voice of America but the Voice of NBC or the Voice of CBS. This arrangement having proved unsatisfactory, the two networks agreed to transfer to the Department as of October 1, 1948, the entire job of broadcasting to Europe and to South America.

Of the other short-term instruments used by the government, the most important are the news bulletins. Some of these go directly to newspaper editors; many more to those who call at the Libraries of Information. This operation, especially in the "gray areas," can be extremely effective, and it is especially needed in areas in which private enterprise is barred.

When our instruments and our methods are compared with those used by the Communists, one wonders how effective ours are.

The American appeal, as made by the government, is directed mainly to the top levels. That is important in its way, because we influence opinion, such as that of editors or leaders in the community, which in turn influences other opinion. But what government is doing is not enough, because it does not reach into a wide enough area and because, owing to the fear of propaganda, the government is likely to pull its punches. It seems clear that new vigor must be added to our appeal and the government's efforts supplemented. That is where private enterprise enters into the picture.

13. The Role of Private Enterprise

The government's effort in the opinion field abroad is widely discussed; the Voice of America operation especially has had a great deal of attention; in general, when there is debate over our propaganda task abroad, the reader thinks first and often exclusively of the government activities.

Yet the role of private enterprise in the job abroad is actually and basically more important and more extensive; that is true even today and, if the operation is developed as it should be, the role will be even greater in the future. For the conception that a European has of the United States is based, in large degree, on what he reads about us in his newspapers, and on the impression he gets from American motion pictures (which comprise approximately 75 percent of the total motion picture coverage of Europe) and from our magazines and books.

Of these private enterprise instruments the news agencies should be rated of prime importance. The Associated Press, the United Press and the International News Service supply American news to hundreds of newspapers abroad. Newspapers on the Continent, however, are usually quite different from the American; they resemble pamphlets or editorial sheets more than news publications. Also European papers are suffering from a paper shortage which may last several years. The result is that space is restricted, and even that space is often devoted to spectacular rather than important news. American news published in the newspapers abroad tends to be of the "yellow" variety, except in Communist newspapers, where it follows the Communist propaganda line. The question is whether the press associations cannot do more to bring about a better balance in, and a de-coloring of, the American news published abroad.

The motion picture, it is obvious, has a huge impact. Our mores, our ambitions, our way of life are assumed to be those we present on the screen. There is little reason for a foreigner to think otherwise—and he doesn't. We ought to recognize as a fact that every film we send abroad is a kind of documentary, whether it is intended to be so or not; even though the subject matter may be incredible crime or complete fantasy, it is presumed that such things can happen here.

The other mass media, magazines and books, also have a vital effect; this is true even of those periodicals printed in English, because there is an increasing amount of English spoken abroad. Moreover a growing number of publishers are putting out foreign editions of magazines or books for European consumption.

For all these instruments of the press—news services, motion pictures, books and periodicals—the question arises as to whether the effort is successful from the propaganda point of view, because, as this writer has tried to make clear, the operation abroad is basically a propaganda operation and all those who engage in it, whether they are members of government or of private industry, must recognize the special responsibilities that are involved.

There is an additional question: whether the government should not make it possible for publishers and movie producers to operate without loss. That is a complicated and highly important issue.[33]

The place of free enterprise in foreign propaganda needs much fuller exploration; it presents many problems[34] but it also offers large opportunities. In all our efforts to influence the attitudes and opinions of peoples in foreign countries, it should be recognized that what we do is more important than what we say, and that it is vital that the Europeans know what we are doing. As the Marshall Plan goes into effect on a large scale, our effort must be redoubled; the government operation needs to be complemented by the efforts of private industry.

14. *A Three-Count Indictment*

Finally, in this survey of the State Department, there is the large and baffling problem of coordination. Two examples taken out of the record of the past year provide highlights for that point—the Palestine and the Smith-Molotov episodes.

The shifts in our Palestine policy—for partition, against partition and then for recognition of partition—supply much ammunition to those who accuse the government of

---

[33] The Foreign Aid Appropriation Act, approved June 28, 1948 (Public Law 472, 80th Congress, Chap. 169, 2nd Session), carried an item of $10 million to guarantee convertibility into dollars of sums received in foreign currencies from the sale of American newspapers, magazines and motion pictures published or produced abroad. The purpose of this guarantee was to make it possible for American enterprises whose receipts had been blocked to continue and to expand their circulation. The first appropriations under this act were made in December 1948.

[34] As Mr. Jackson points out in Chapter Nine.

the lack of a foreign policy. It is true that conditions changed greatly between the time of the vote for partition in November 1947 and the meeting of the Assembly four months later; that the Russian threat had become, or we thought it had become, much more serious; that domestic political considerations were reappraised more carefully in the light of what was deemed to be the overriding national interest. Yet, despite all these extenuating factors, there still stands out a strange record of backing and filling, virtually in the public view, and an obvious failure to provide to the public and the press a sufficient or even coherent statement of the reasons for these changes.

The Smith-Molotov episode, months after it took place, still remained a mystery. What seemed clear was that the Russians had taken advantage of a vulnerable tactic on our part and used it as the focal point of a propaganda drive. As *The Economist* put it, Molotov had succeeded in turning an *aide-mémoire* into a *billet doux*. And again the press and the people were left in the dark as to our motives and our objectives. The white-shuttered curtain was again drawn.

Episodes like these, which seem to increase in frequency with the increase in the complexity of world problems, lead to a good deal of eyebrow-raising when the question of the efficiency of the State Department is under discussion. Five years ago a former member of the Department wrote:

> The Department is an unbelievably inefficient organization. It is not run. It just jerks along. Foreign policy is in the hands of whichever of two dozen higher officers is able at any moment and by any means to seize the ball. But in the State Department there are queer rules: when a player seizes the ball and makes for the goal line, all the members of his team are entitled to tackle him. And as often as not the ball is seized and not carried over any goal line but hidden under the back steps.[35]

As of today this is surely an overstatement. Yet the State Department, on the issue of coordination, is still indicted on these counts:

[35] Joseph M. Jones, *op. cit.,* p. 37.

1. That there is an insufficient amount of planning in the Department. Until recently only the Secretary, the Under-Secretary and the Counselor were in a position to consider our foreign policy as a whole; now there is, in addition, the Planning Group; but in practice all three officials, and the planners as well, are bogged down in the detail of the Department.

2. That the lines of responsibility are not clearly drawn. Subordinate officers, fearful of treading upon sensitive toes, or of getting out on one of the many limbs of the huge Department tree, check and counter-check, seek to avoid responsibility by adding a slew of initials to every document.

3. That coordination is lacking among the rapidly multiplying divisions and officers, each not infrequently ignorant of what others are doing. The liaison could be established through the upper echelons, but the men there are so concerned with the grinding pressures of events, or with appearances before Congressional committees, or with public engagements, that they cannot carry through the assignment.

Efforts are now being made to reorganize the Department, to cut the red tape, and to set a sharper pattern of responsibility. There have been efforts in the past, many investigations. The results have been summed up, possibly with more acid than accuracy, in these words: "These investigators start out with hopes of finding an exact formula for making policy and they end up by recommending improvement in the messenger service. No matter what their objectives, they always come back to those poor messengers."

Now there are new efforts and new hopes that important improvements will be effected, that there will be much more than betterment of the messenger service. Secretary Acheson brings to bear on these problems both experience and understanding. But the difficulties of the task should not be underestimated; there are high hurdles of tradition, of inertia, of resistance that must be cleared.[36]

---

[36] With the publication of the reports of the Commission on Organization of

15. The Three Basic Problems

In sum, then, the basic problems that confront government in its public opinion operations are these:

The Problem of Education: We are faced with the task of building a better informed opinion. That means, on the government's part, a clear and courageous definition of its job and a new and vigorous drive to inform the nation and to persuade the world; on the part of the people, an understanding of the task and full support of it.

The Problem of Implementation: Public opinion is not easily measured and interpreted; that requires special skills and techniques. The public opinion job cannot be done by amateurs or simple do-gooders; it calls for a sophisticated group of experts—and sophistication does not exclude sincerity. This means more adequate support from Congress.

The Problem of Coordination: We have four main government groups concerned with public opinion in foreign affairs—the President, the Congress, the Defense Departments and the State Department—and it is conceivable that there might be four policies on a single issue. Obviously greater direction and synchronization are required if the nation shall not be bewildered and the rest of the world made cynical.

The chapters that follow discuss in detail these three problems and point the way to possible solutions. The discussion is in two parts: Part I is a description and evaluation of the public opinion operation at home; Part II is a description and evaluation of the public opinion operation abroad.

This introduction has been an attempt only to set out the picture in perspective; the panorama is a large one and on

---

the Executive Branch of the Government, of which Mr. Herbert Hoover is chairman (to be issued about the same time that this book is published), these questions will have increased attention. The Commission makes a number of drastic recommendations for the reorganization of the State Department. Mr. Acheson was Vice Chairman of that Commission, and there is every indication that many of the recommendations will be adopted.

the limited canvas of a single book one can hope at best to capture only part of it. But if this volume succeeds in persuading the reader of the present neglect and the future importance of the public opinion task, then its authors believe that it will have done a major service.

PART ONE

FOREIGN POLICY AND OPINION AT HOME

These chapters evaluate the public opinion problem at home; they indicate the proportions of the problem; they describe the opinion operation as it is carried on by the main government branches concerned with it—the President, the Congress, the Military, the Department of State; they appraise the effectiveness of the operation; and they make some suggestions for its improvement.

CHAPTER TWO

DARK AREAS OF IGNORANCE

By Martin Kriesberg

THERE ARE 148,000,000 Americans. These are the people who ultimately make or break our foreign policy. They are conglomerate; among them approximately fifty racial and national groups are represented. Their emotions and thinking are influenced by many factors—geographical, educational, economic, religious, ethnical. All these factors add to the complexity of the task of building an intelligent foreign policy which will have the solid support of a majority of the people. Yet our policy must have widespread popular support if it is to be democratic in concept and effective in action.

The task of educating and informing American public opinion in the field of foreign affairs is complex. First, we must analyze the state of public information; we have to find out what people know and what they do not know, to map the areas of ignorance. Second, we must examine popular prejudices based on misinformation. Third, we must find out where people get their information, or misinformation, about foreign affairs. With this background we can proceed to assess the effects on foreign policy of lack of information, misinformation and prejudice, and to consider what can be done to achieve a better informed opinion.

1. *The Aware and the Unaware*

There are some general clues as to the extent of the areas of ignorance and apathy in the nation. We have, for example, data on education and on the exercise of the voting franchise.

According to the census of 1940, six out of ten Americans, 25 years of age or over, had never gone beyond the eighth school grade. This is the picture:

Persons in the U. S. 25 years of age or over	73,691,000
Persons who never completed one school year	2,800,000
Persons who completed grades 1 to 4	7,305,000
Persons who completed grades 5 to 6	8,515,000
Persons who completed grades 7 to 8	25,898,000
Persons who completed high school years 1 to 3	11,182,000
Persons who completed 4th year of high school	10,552,000
Persons who completed 1 to 3 years of college	3,407,000
Persons who completed 4 or more years of college	1,042,000
Median school years completed	8.4

Apathy in citizenship was never more clearly demonstrated than in the recent Presidential election. Despite the fact that the nation was facing great domestic and foreign problems, only 49,000,000 of 95,000,000 eligible voters went to the polls. A study of election charts since 1912 reveals that, in general, only 50 percent of those eligible vote in Presidential elections. These statistics are not encouraging to the future of democracy.

There are also specific clues as to the areas of ignorance; these are based on the findings of the polls. Some harsh words have been spoken in recent months about the polls. Yet, if they are conducted properly and if the data are interpreted with due regard to the limitations of the material, polls are invaluable sources of information on many issues.[1] One of the uses of poll material is to disclose the areas of ignorance—and that is the particular concern of this chapter. If there is any error in the polls' reports on the extent

---

[1] I am much more doubtful on this score than Mr. Kriesberg (see pp. 30-31), but only time will resolve this particular debate.—L. M.

of popular ignorance, it is likely to be in reporting a higher level of information in the electorate than actually exists. People are prone to imply that they are better informed than in fact they are, because to admit ignorance might mean losing face with the interviewer. Moreover, if a sampling error occurs in polls, it is likely to be in the direction of oversampling the better educated and better informed segments of the population. Accordingly, a report on areas of public ignorance on world affairs, to the extent that it is based on poll data, probably presents a conservative estimate.

What, then, do the polls disclose about popular knowledge of foreign policy? Those who analyze and interpret polls classify people in three categories: (1) the *unaware,* the people who freely confess that they have neither heard nor read of important issues in American foreign policy; (2) the *aware,* the people who have heard or read the issues but who have only rudimentary knowledge about them; (3) the *informed,* the people who are not only *aware* of the issues but who also know their meaning and their implications. Usually both the *unaware* and the *aware* are regarded as *uninformed.* Using these definitions public opinion analysts over a period of years have established the following:

> About 30 percent of the electorate, on the average, is *unaware* of almost any given event in American foreign affairs.
>
> About 45 percent of the electorate is *aware* of important events in the field but cannot be considered *informed.* These people retain little information. Although they may follow discussions of the issues of foreign policy, they cannot frame intelligent arguments about them.
>
> Only 25 percent of the electorate consistently shows knowledge of foreign problems.

These averages do not hold for all issues. When an aspect of foreign policy is the big news of the moment, the number of the *unaware* is likely to drop somewhat, and the number of the *aware* but *uninformed,* as well as the number of the *informed,* will increase. But even when an issue has received widespread publicity, a large proportion of the electorate remains unaware of it, and substantially less than half is found to be *informed.* For example, the following table indicates the state of public understanding (and, more importantly, of public ignorance) on three much publicized issues of recent years.

TABLE I

STATE OF PUBLIC INFORMATION ON THREE
FOREIGN POLICY ISSUES

Issue	Unaware	Uninformed Aware	Informed
		(Percentages)	
The British Loan Proposal (March 1946)	15	60	25
The Greek-Turkish Aid Proposal (March 1947)	16	47	37
The Marshall Plan Proposal (February 1948)	16	70	14 [2]

These statistics indicate the extent of the widespread political ignorance with which we must contend. People who lack information on foreign affairs tend to be uninformed on domestic affairs. But there is an important difference: the polls indicate that, while the degree of unawareness is about the same for domestic and foreign affairs, fewer persons are informed on foreign affairs. In a number of surveys by Dr Gallup's American Institute of Public Opinion, less than one fourth of the voters showed enough knowledge to rate a

[2] As the Marshall Plan discussion proceeded, the number of those informed was, of course, increased, but at no time did it reach a figure that could be called encouraging.

informed on foreign affairs, and on domestic issues about one-third.[3]

Being aware of an event seems to require only exposure (e.g., through newspapers or the radio), whereas being informed requires an active interest. People are more interested in domestic affairs because they directly affect their lives; foreign affairs seem remote. When asked what specific issues interested them, 67 percent of the electorate mentioned such things as inflation control and food shortages, while only 60 percent mentioned issues of foreign policy, such as atomic control and relations with Russia. Similarly, people talk more about domestic than foreign matters. Approximately 45 percent of the voters reported that they discussed domestic issues, while only 36 percent said they discussed foreign policy issues.[4]

[3] The topics on foreign and domestic affairs (and the date the survey was made) were:

Foreign: Ruling power in Palestine, December 1944
Yalta Conference, March 1945
San Francisco Conference, April 1945
Nature of Bretton Woods Proposals, May 1945
Voting procedure in U. N. Security Council, July 1945
Terms of Lend-lease agreements, October 1945
Churchill's speech at Fulton, Missouri, March 1946
The loan to Britain, April 1946
Paris Peace Conference, June 1946
Civil strife in China, August 1946
President Truman's Greece-Turkey speech, March 1947

Domestic: Government seizure of Montgomery Ward plant, May 1944
President Roosevelt's proposal for National Service Law, February 1945
Purpose of the "Little Steel Formula," April 1945
Functions of the T.V.A., May 1945
Functions of the O.W.I., June 1945
Veteran election in Athens, Tennessee, September 1946
Provisions of the Wagner Labor Act, January 1947
Meaning of "portal to portal pay," January 1947
Dispute over governor in Georgia, February 1947
Confirmation of Lilienthal appointment to Atomic Energy Commission, February 1947
Taft-Hartley Labor Bill, August 1947

[4] The topics upon which these averages were computed were:

Foreign: Control of the atomic bomb   27%
Shipments of food and relief to Europe   46%
Relations with Russia   35%   Average 36%

When information is related to personal or group interest, it is more readily understood and retained. For example, 80 percent of the people were able to give reasonable arguments for continuing the OPA; only 44 percent could give reasonable arguments for making the British loan. In the same way, while 66 percent could give cogent reasons against continuing OPA, only 49 percent supplied reasons for opposing the British loan.

There are definite areas of ignorance in the popular mind which are traceable to social, economic, educational and geographical conditions. In this connection Table II (on the opposite page) is revealing.

This breakdown of the areas of ignorance throws much light on the problem of educating public opinion. It is worth while to look separately at the differences in each category.

Sex. Of 45 million women eligible to vote, some 38 million are uninformed about the most important issues and events in American foreign policy; almost 10 million never even heard or read about them. For example, 19 percent of the women polled, compared with 13 percent of the men, had never heard of the Marshall Plan. Only 12 percent of the women polled could state its purpose.

Income. The lower a person's income the less is his information. Eighty-eight percent of voters with less-than-average incomes, compared to 82 percent with above-average incomes, could not cite the purpose of the Marshall Plan. Why are the poor more uninformed? Primarily because they lack the interest, the time and the background to become informed. Few of them consider knowledge of foreign affairs either necessary or helpful. One unskilled worker replied to an interviewer, "Foreign affairs! That's for people who don't have to work for a living."

Domestic:	The housing shortage	65%	
	The federal government's budget	34%	
	Labor problems	40%	Average 45%

TABLE II

LEVELS OF INFORMATION ON THE MARSHALL PLAN[5]

Categories:	Informed — Gave reasonably accurate statement of purposes of Plan	Uninformed — Aware — Thought it meant "Just help Europe"	Uninformed — Aware — Didn't know its purpose	Uninformed — Unaware — Had never heard or read anything about the Marshall Plan
	(Percentages)			
Sex				
Men	16	60	11	13
Women	12	49	20	19
Income				
Wealthy	18	72	7	3
Average	15	64	12	9
Poor	12	44	21	23
Education				
College	20	69	8	3
High school	17	53	16	14
Grammar school or less	10	41	20	29
Rural-Urban				
Farm and rural	13	54	15	18
Town and small city	14	53	16	17
Metropolitan city	18	54	14	14
Region				
New England	16	59	10	15
Mid-Atlantic	17	53	15	15
Central	13	52	17	18
South and southwest	12	52	16	20
Mountain and Pacific	17	55	14	14

[5] Based on a Gallup Poll, February 1948.

Education. About 29 percent of Americans with grammar schooling or less are unaware of the Marshall Plan, compared with 3 percent of the college graduates. The uneducated are, by and large, the same persons who fall into the low-income group. Their ignorance can be explained partly by their occupations and partly by their lack of facility in reading and in piecing together the information they obtain either from newspapers or the radio. Hence, they accept without question the simpler, and often the more superficial, reporting on foreign matters.

Rural-urban. Urban residents are generally better informed than people in the country for a variety of reasons. Educational facilities are frequently better in the cities. Cities prosper on commerce, which is itself a branch of foreign affairs. Often, as we shall see later, the channels of information, newspapers, radio, television, are more accessible and do a better job of information in the cities.

Region. The regional data confirm generally accepted notions. Persons living on the West and East Coasts seem to be better informed than those in the Midwest and in Southern hinterlands. On the coasts, where the ties to foreign lands are more keenly felt, people take a greater interest in international affairs than in the hinterland. You may argue that agricultural prosperity depends on foreign trade, but it is still hard to persuade the Middle West farmer that he is concerned with what goes on in Trieste. Three thousand miles of water plus 1,500 miles of American soil give him, in spite of the atom bomb, a sense of security. In the South, information is less than in the coastal regions, owing to poorer educational facilities and a lower standard of living.

Out of this survey there emerges this impression and this depressing fact: that in general the number of those informed on questions of foreign policy is no greater than the number of those who are totally unaware. And it must be kept in mind that the polls tend to overestimate the voters' store of information.

2. *Areas of Prejudice*

Not only widespread ignorance but deep-seated prejudices hinder the emergence of an informed public opinion on issues of foreign policy. Today three widely held prejudices, beliefs based on feeling rather than reason, are influencing our policy: (1) Many Americans have a strong spirit of chauvinism; they are convinced that we are the most righteous and mightiest of all peoples. (2) Many are prone to deep-rooted isolationism, arising from a mistaken belief in the self-sufficiency of America. (3) Many are convinced that America is the most generous of nations and that what help we give abroad comes under the heading of charity—Christian charity is the term.

Chauvinism, as the name implies, is not peculiarly American. Like peoples in other lands, the American takes pride in his history. He regards his country as the most enlightened, the best governed, the most just in the world. According to Professor Bailey, "The more ignorant the citizen, the more bellicose and jingoistic [he is] . . . the more certain that we could knock the stuffings out of any or all other nations."[6]

This long-cherished notion of rectitude and superiority naturally colors our attitudes toward foreign countries. The feeling that as a nation we can do no wrong tends to make us uncritical of our policies toward other peoples. When foreigners object to American policies, our probable reaction is not to reexamine the American position but to reject categorically the foreign criticism.

Isolation is an understandable by-product of American history. The great majority of early settlers came here to get away from Europe and Europe's problems. They wanted to forget Europe and to get along by themselves. America's size and vast resources made such a prospect plausible. With the radio and the airplane circumstances have changed, but

---

[6] Thomas E. Bailey, *op. cit.*, p. 134.

the old isolationism persists. Moreover, the uninformed fail to recognize that wealth and strength do not make America self-sufficient. They forget how hard our economy was hit in World War II when the Japanese conquests in the Far East cut off rubber, quinine and vegetable oils.

Belief in America's self-sufficiency affects the way we behave toward other peoples. We hesitate to make common cause with other nations, and we are reluctant to make concessions to them. When we encounter differences with other powers, we prefer to withdraw into isolation rather than seek a basis for cooperation. If we have little to gain by collaboration, why compromise our position for the advantages of others?

The American penchant for charity on an international plane is almost as old as the Republic. Its roots are in religion and these roots have been nurtured by American missionaries for more than a century. Their efforts—the schools and hospitals they have built abroad, for example—have produced much good will toward this country. But here at home the false notion has arisen that all American assistance to foreign peoples comes solely under the heading of charity.

Uninformed Americans, still regarding our shipments of wheat and machines as pure charity, expect foreign lands to accept our aid gratefully. They do not understand why recipient governments overseas should have any say about the terms under which the help is granted. If, as Table II indicates, great numbers of our people regard the Marshall Plan solely as a helping hand to Europe, they are consequently unable to understand the European concern over the conditions that we might attach to our aid.

These prejudices are responsible for strong pressures on government to adopt courses that the men in charge of our foreign policy regard as wrong. For example, immediately after Pearl Harbor the widespread and almost personal

Dark Areas of Ignorance

hatred of the average American for the Japanese, strengthened by the feeling that the United States had been dealt a foul blow, stimulated strong demands that the U. S. attack in the Pacific first and take on Germany later. The history of the war indicates that the government's course in resisting this pressure was correct.

When prejudice is added to ignorance, the sum constitutes a dark area in which acute dangers may breed. It becomes important, therefore, to identify the sources of these dangers so that we can make the effort to overcome or at least to lessen them—to try to discover where we acquire our knowledge and impressions of world affairs.

3. *Our Sources of Information*

Americans get their information (and misinformation) from a variety of sources. There is the ancient avenue of word of mouth. About one in ten Americans admits that most of his information comes from discussions with friends and relatives. Then there is the avenue of the mass organization. More than one-half of the American people belong to organized religious bodies and attend their services; 15 million persons belong to trade unions; 5 million to veterans' organizations; several million more to fraternal and other group societies. Most important of all, there is the press—the organized, commercial channels of mass communication.

Americans read a greater number of newspapers and magazines, own more radio sets and see more motion pictures than do any other people in the world. More than 80 percent of the voters are reached by both radio and newspaper. In 1947 approximately 40 million homes in the United States, more than 94 percent of all homes, had radio sets. Two-thirds of the people listen to radio newscasts regularly. Newspapers also have a large audience; 80 percent of the people read a daily or weekly newspaper regularly. About 50 percent of the people read magazines; books have a large public, aided by book clubs and pocket editions. Motion pictures and newsreels have a weekly audience, including repeaters, of almost a hundred million adults.

For their news on foreign affairs, more than 90 percent of the population depends principally on two sources, the radio and the daily newspaper. The radio, although a newer medium, exerts a powerful influence. Analyses of polls indicate that a majority of Americans have a general preference for radio as a source of information on foreign affairs. For opinion as contrasted with news, radio commentators are considerably more popular than newspaper columnists; 39 percent of those polled favor them, and only 11 percent indicate that they prefer to read interpretations of the news.

According to the polls, radio is the medium most trusted by a majority of Americans. A *Fortune* survey in August 1939 reported that 50 percent of the people thought the air waves were freer from prejudice than the newspapers; only 17 percent championed the latter. In the event of conflicting news reports, a plurality of respondents was inclined to accept the radio version. In 1945, the National Opinion Research Center reported that 46 percent felt radio to be more accurate while only 29 percent thought newspapers more trustworthy.[7]

The preference for radio is particularly pronounced among the lower income groups and the less educated, among women and unskilled workers, among rural residents and among the foreign born. Such preference stems logically from less familiarity with the printed word and less willingness to expend effort in learning about world affairs.

On the other hand, newspapers take precedence in the

[7] I do not accept these surveys as fully as Mr. Kriesberg does. The subject of trustworthiness is one which deserves more extended consideration. In some surveys the issue becomes confused in the minds of those polled. For example, the pollees are asked: "Do you depend on the newspaper or the radio for the news?" In many cases the question is understood to mean: "Which medium brings the news to you sooner?" Obviously, the answer is the radio. In any case the prime source of news for the radio is the same as that for the newspaper—the news agency.—L. M.

higher income groups which comprise the better educated sections of the population and also the groups which are most concerned about foreign affairs—the influential citizens, the civic leaders. Although influenced, often more than they like to admit, by their favorite radio commentators, these people rely more than other groups on newspapers to keep them in touch with what is going on in the world. Through them outstanding newspapers exert an influence on public opinion out of proportion to their circulation figures.

The responsibility of the press in the United States, particularly the radio and the newspapers, in the field of public education can hardly be exaggerated. To a considerable extent they can bring about, or prevent, an enlightened public opinion.

How well has the press discharged its responsibility? The answer is "not too well." The desire to sell their wares has a powerful influence on the selection of what newspapers print and on the programs of radio stations. Although there are publishers and radio stations that try to fulfill their responsibilities faithfully, the tendency in too much of the press is to try to please as many people as possible. On this point the Commission on Freedom of the Press has said:

Information and discussion regarding public affairs, carried as a rider on the omnibus of mass communication, take on the character of the other passengers and become subject to the same laws that governed their selection; such information and discussion must be shaped so that they will pay their own way by attracting the maximum audience.[8]

The radio, as we have seen, is the principal source of foreign news for a great part of the electorate. Yet, few of these listeners hear the serious programs provided by radio round-tables and forums; less than two-thirds of them regularly listen to news reports. Radio news reports are brief, and besides only a fraction of each report is devoted to foreign affairs.

[8] *A Free and Responsible Press, op. cit.,* p. 54.

Although more than 80 percent of the American people regularly read newspapers, only 50 percent spend a half hour or more in perusing them. In this brief space the reading is likely to be superficial; foreign news may be passed over entirely or given merely a cursory glance. Also, many people have time to read only one newspaper, and thus have no basis for judging either the adequacy or the objectivity of its foreign coverage.

Moreover, the press generally gives its readers too little information about what is going on abroad, or about the problems with which the State Department has to deal. Also, too many newspapers and radio programs, when they do treat foreign affairs, emphasize feeling and emotion rather than thought and reason.

If the American press is asked why, with its multiple information channels and its mass coverage, it has not contributed more to popular education in foreign affairs, the first answer is that the people are not interested.

Thus we seem to be caught in a vicious circle. Newspapers do not emphasize foreign affairs because the people are not interested, and the people are not interested because they do not find much foreign news in their papers.

In this connection, the political apathy of the uninformed is an important factor. The uninformed usually believe that no political event can greatly affect their personal fortunes. While foreign policy issues agitate the informed, the world of the uninformed is circumscribed by the daily cares of a child's cough, a boss's gripe, an unexpected frost. They are too immersed in the details of daily living to make the effort to inform themselves on what is happening in Yugoslavia or Germany. They are even less concerned about communicating their views to Congress because they believe that their views are not taken into account by the government. Why should they take the trouble to keep informed on foreign policies?

But the facts are otherwise, and they must be driven home. What happens in any quarter of the world has an effect on the life of even the humblest citizen, and he must be made to realize it. An uninformed electorate acts as a drag upon the government. Prejudices which fetter the ignorant and apathetic voters hang heavily upon the hands of their representatives also. Policies designed to meet new conditions run counter to old concepts which are cherished by the uninformed. Therein lies the danger.

4. The Remedies

What's to be done? How can apathy and indifference be transformed into active interest in foreign affairs? How can ignorant and prejudiced people be transformed into a well-informed, tolerant electorate?

All this, as was said in the first chapter, is part of the general problem of education—and that is not the main theme of this book. It has been considered in this chapter solely to emphasize its great importance and to keep the picture in perspective.

In the long run, the remedies for ignorance and prejudice must be found in education on a broad scale and among all classes, and particularly in the improvement of the economic and social position of the lower income groups.

But we are continually reminded that the pressure of events, the issues of foreign and domestic policy, demand decisions today, not fifty years hence. We must act, here and now, to promote among the people of the world a clearer appreciation of the role of the United States in world affairs, a better understanding of the consequences that will result from failure to fulfill the role.

We must bring light into the areas of ignorance. All the media of mass education, all the media of mass communication must be mobilized for the effort; the school, the college, the public forum, the press must all do their part.

Government, too, must do its part—on its own and in cooperation with these other instruments of enlightenment. What that part can be is indicated in the chapters that follow.

CHAPTER THREE

THE NUMBER ONE VOICE

By James Reston

THE PRESIDENT of the United States influences opinion by every public act. The soldiers and the diplomats may or may not command the attention of the people by what they say or do, but the electorate is never indifferent to the slightest activity in the White House. No matter who he is, the President is a symbol of his office and his country. Even the least competent chief executive is the successor of Washington and Lincoln. Consequently, when he speaks, he speaks for America, he influences the lives of Americans, he represents or misrepresents the ideal every man has in his mind of what the President should say or do, and for these reasons, men listen when he speaks.

Moreover, the whole apparatus of the most modern and extensive system of rapid communications ever gathered together in one country is constantly at his disposal. Everything he says or does is news. If he goes to Congress to address the federal legislature, the major radio networks record every word and the television cameras transmit every flicker and expression of his face. If he goes to the country for the week end, he is followed by a battery of reporters and cameramen. If he gets a new dog, or expresses a preference for a picture, or has a daughter who sings, or acquires a new gadget for his desk, the object of his interest is subjected to the same careful scrutiny as a new policy sent to Congress.

The fierce competition of the private agencies gathering

and disseminating news provides the President with a ready audience on almost every occasion. He is the "big story." Only a few papers and agencies assign reporters to the State Department and the Defense Departments in Washington, but almost all are represented at the White House. Whenever the President holds a press conference, at least 150 reporters attend.

The competition is so sharp that, when the press conference ends, the scramble of reporters for the telephones is a menace to life and limb, and this competition to report what the President says is not restricted to the representatives of press associations, newspapers and the radio. The magazine writers, the newsreel reporters, and even the book publishers are equally eager to have access to material, critical or merely descriptive, about the President and his administration. The President, consequently, more than any member of his administration or any political competitor, because of the preeminence of his office and the competition of the various news agencies, can be assured of getting his views before the people whenever he likes.

He can, for example, appoint committees to study the question at issue and release their findings to the public. On the basis of the study he can have legislation prepared and send it to Congress with a message stating or re-stating his reasons for wishing action. He can go personally to Congress and address both houses in joint session if he believes the matter at issue warrants such dramatic action. He can arrange to make a public speech on the subject whenever he chooses, or simply ask for radio time in order to carry his argument to the people. He can comment on the question at his meetings with the press and radio reporters. He can take it up with his Cabinet, authorizing them to discuss the question openly on Capitol Hill or in public speeches. He can have a message prepared for the newsreel cameras and either deliver the message himself or arrange to have it delivered by some prominent government official.

The President of the United States, in short, is in a unique position to influence the views of his fellow citizens: he is part symbol, part executive, part actor, part "graven image." No man in history ever had such an opportunity to reach so many people so quickly, and so often, with the assurance of an attentive audience as he. That is why, in any study of public opinion in the United States, it is vital to survey the influences that play upon the President and the uses he makes of his great power.

1. *The Growth of the President's Influence*

In the early days of the Republic, modern techniques for influencing opinion were not available. The President's influence over the mass of people not only was restricted by space and poor communications, but also by suffrage restrictions which left the business of government in the hands of something approaching a governing class. This situation was not offensive to the aristocratic views of the early Presidents. But Jefferson was an exception; he wrote to Edward Carrington:

... the people are the only censors of their governors. ... The way to prevent these irregular interpositions of the people, is to give them full information of their affairs thro' the channel of the public papers, & to contrive that those papers should penetrate the whole mass of the people. The basis of our governments being the opinion of the people, the very first object should be to keep that right; and were it left to me to decide whether we should have a government without newspapers, or newspapers without a government, I should not hesitate a moment to prefer the latter. But I should mean that every man should receive those papers, and be capable of reading them.[1]

When Lincoln became President, the United States under the influence of the frontier had made long strides in the direction of democratic self-government. More than any of his predecessors in the office, more than many of his suc-

---
[1] Quoted in James E. Pollard, *The Presidents and the Press,* New York, Macmillan, 1947, pp. 52-53.

cessors, Lincoln recognized the power of public opinion. George Fort Milton has written:

> None have surpassed Lincoln, and few have equaled him as Chief of Public Opinion, a role as unknown to the Constitution as the equally unofficial headship of the party which nominates him for President. . . .
> From inauguration until assassination, he always tried to inform the people of some among the controlling reasons for his policies and acts. While he paid some heed to the sanctity of military secrets, he declined to worship at that shrine. He knew that people had ears, whether the walls had them or not, and took advantage of every appropriate occasion to tell them his innermost thoughts. . . . He seldom made a move without explaining its purpose, and often outlining the whole background of events which had forced the action. He frequently used a particular power right to the limit, but never without letting the people know why circumstances had forced this to be done for the public good.[2]

Presidents coming after Lincoln varied widely in their ability to understand and to guide public opinion. Hayes had "a strong sense of public relations and a good appreciation of the importance of sound public opinion."[3] Cleveland despite his great abilities as a statesman seemed unable to deal effectively with public opinion. Theodore Roosevelt took full advantage of the publicity value of his colorful personality. His shrewdness in dealing with the press enabled him to put his views effectively before the people. Woodrow Wilson, because he wanted to take the people into his confidence, was the first President to hold press conferences regularly. "Few Presidents before him," writes Pollard, "and only one or two since have been as aware of public opinion and the important relationship of the press thereto as Woodrow Wilson."[4] Until the latter part of his second administration President Wilson, although he did not cultivate a wide variety of contacts, was remarkably sensitive to the trend of popular thinking and feeling:

---
[2] *The Use of Presidential Powers,* Boston, Little, Brown, 1944, p. 131.
[3] Pollard, *op. cit.,* p. 476.
[4] *Ibid.,* p. 690.

His general knowledge of the character and thought of the people and their historical tendencies coupled with an almost uncanny ability to sense the aspirations of the people seems to have accounted for his ability to crystallize public opinion and express the common feeling in clear and striking fashion.[5]

Wilson's failure in his fight to bring the United States into the League of Nations showed that he had lost the close touch with public opinion which was so great a source of strength in earlier years.

The late President Franklin Roosevelt and his press secretary, Steve Early, developed these possibilities to a greater degree than any other Washington administration. They were the perfect combination: Roosevelt had the voice for radio, the looks for the camera, the skill of a parliamentarian in answering questions. Early was a good technician, well trained in the needs of correspondents, capable of translating the activities of government into news, shrewd at judging those correspondents who could be trusted and those who couldn't and, with a keen sense of timing, quick to sense when the public wished to hear from the President.

Even Early did not make the most of his own or his boss's possibilities, but he came closer to developing a scientific approach to influencing public opinion than any other employee at the White House since President Wilson inaugurated the regular White House press conference.

Roosevelt introduced the "fireside chat"—the casual informal radio talk to the people in their homes. He chose occasions when they needed guidance on difficult issues, and selected hours when they were most likely to listen in.

All Presidents, however, do not have the "Roosevelt touch" with correspondents. President Truman has adopted the casual Rooseveltian manner in his press conferences, but he has never used the conferences as effectively, and he has seldom attempted the fireside chat technique. The Truman

---

[5] Charles W. Smith, *Public Opinion in a Democracy*, New York, Prentice-Hall, 1939, p. 196.

technique, especially during the Presidential campaign of 1948, was in some ways more effective out of Washington than in the capital. When he was formal, he could not duplicate the success of Roosevelt, but as a casual spokesman for himself, speaking directly to the people as his train crossed the country, he was exceptionally provocative and persuasive.

2. *How the President Gauges Opinion*

The occupant of the White House is supposed to have a lonely job, cut off from the pressure of outside opinion, aloof from the freely expressed views of average citizens, and surrounded by yes-men who hesitate to give him a critical analysis of his failings. There is some danger here, but there are ways of minimizing it. The President has unique opportunities to gather information about what the people are thinking. For one thing, the President has access to the studies of public opinion and to the public opinion polls, for such value as they may have. He can, if he likes, have additional surveys made.

Most Presidents have been avid newspaper readers. President Roosevelt had the capacity of scanning half a dozen metropolitan dailies before getting out of bed in the morning and of retaining all the pertinent information they contained. Mr. Truman is not so accomplished a newspaper reader, but he goes through several papers in an average day and in addition keeps abreast of the current flow of events by means of a news ticker installed in the White House press room. The latest news is brought to him throughout the day in short "takes" which he reads whenever he has a free moment. One function of his Press Secretary is to clip and place on his desk particularly significant news items and editorials from papers which the President does not ordinarily see. During much of the New Deal an elaborate central clipping bureau was maintained which studied more than 500 daily and weekly papers, not only for White House consumption but for the benefit of the executive departments as well. Weekly "box scores" of editorial opinion, broken down geographically and by subject matter, were sent regularly to the White House.

On items of particular pertinency, the President may have special studies made by members of his staff or Cabinet. Officials in various federal field offices from one end of the continent to the other may be tapped for public attitudes in their localities on a given policy or proposal, and asked to report the pro's and con's as they find them locally. Or, as has happened on several occasions, the President may send out a scout, perhaps incognito, to take the public pulse on a given issue. The establishment of a system of transient shelters early in the New Deal resulted from a "bumming" trip across the country by George Allen, disguised as a jobless wanderer, at the behest of President Roosevelt.

Before launching his slashing attack against the Eightieth Congress during the recent Presidential campaign, President Truman had his long-time confidant, Leslie Biffle, tour the rural districts of several Midwestern states in the guise of a poultry buyer. With an aged truck and a stack of chicken crates aboard, the usually immaculate Mr. Biffle, dressed in rough work clothes, talked with hundreds of farmers and small-town merchants about chickens and politics, but mostly politics. At the same time, and in somewhat less dramatic fashion, Under-Secretary of the Interior Oscar Chapman toured the Far Western states sounding out local politicos on what sort of campaign the President should wage. David Niles, an executive assistant to both Presidents Roosevelt and Truman, has spent almost as much time outside of Washington as he has in it during the last six years, maintaining contact with the principal minority groups of the country and funneling their sentiments and reactions into the White House.

Most official callers at the White House are regarded

skeptically as purveyors of intelligence on public opinion. There is a tendency among most people to tell so exalted a host as the President of the United States, not the harsh and perhaps unpleasant facts of life, but a glossed-up version designed to please or flatter. There are exceptions, of course, whom the President and his staff quickly learn to recognize as reliable. Often they are accorded off-the-record conferences with the President, entering through the East Wing where reporters do not keep a vigil, and being permitted to remain considerably beyond the usual 15- or 20-minute visit. From such visitors as these, a President can often gain fresh and revealing slants on public attitudes not available from official and semi-official sources.

Consultations with members of Congress are a less fruitful means of guidance on public opinion than they would appear to be on the surface. There are a variety of reasons for this. President Roosevelt, for example, felt there was little that any Congressman could tell him about public opinion that he did not already know. Sometimes he was right about this, and sometimes wrong, as his ill-fated attempt in 1938 to purge certain Congressmen showed.

On the other hand President Truman, an alumnus of the Senate, where he served for ten years before becoming Vice President, has frequently consulted Congressmen privately. The President has friendly relations with many of the leading Senators, who were in the upper chamber when he was there. On several occasions he has gone from the White House to lunch in the Senate dining room. Undoubtedly these contacts have been of value to him.

Through all these channels Presidents, therefore, are able to keep abreast of the nation's thinking and to guide their policy by what they learn. But in the effort to use this knowledge to win support for their policies, other factors make for or against success. Of these factors the two most important are (a) press relations and (b) coordination within the executive departments.

3. The President's Relations with the Press

The personal relationship between the President and the working press has an indirect but important bearing on the dissemination of White House news and therefore on public opinion. No matter how honestly a reporter may strive for accuracy and objectivity in his coverage of news, he is, after all, a human being who responds emotionally to human traits and characteristics in the people on whom he reports. By unconscious nuances and inflections, by unintentional semantic shadings in his copy, he can scarcely avoid sympathetic treatment of a subject he likes, or unsympathetic treatment of one he does not. This varies in great degree among reporters, but it is true to some extent of all of them. In consequence, Herbert Hoover, for example, whose relations with reporters were notably cool, found very few of them in his corner when he needed them during the closing months of his administration. The hostility which his personal aloofness had inspired was intensified by his insistence that press conference questions be presented in advance in writing. Roosevelt went to the opposite extreme, both in his personal relationships with reporters and in the free-style system which he adopted for press conferences. The reaction against the New Deal that began to set in after 1938 would certainly have gone much deeper, it seems reasonable to believe, if FDR had been less personable and persuasive.

President Truman has demonstrated some of the same capacity for attracting the sympathy of the White House correspondents, and he benefits accordingly in their treatment of him. This was most forcefully demonstrated during the 1948 Presidential campaign when, in literally hundreds of dispatches from the candidates' trains, the notion was firmly implanted in the public mind of Truman's warm and human qualities as opposed to the aloofness and impersonal efficiency of his opponent, Governor Dewey.

But good personal relations with the working press are

not enough. Much, of course, depends on how the President uses the news-making possibilities of his office, coordinating his actions with important developments elsewhere in the capital. Studies of the news-reading habits of the American people indicate, for example, that they can digest only one big news story at a time. It is, therefore, in the interest of the Executive not to release too many important stories at once, and not to announce new policies at a time when they are likely to be overwhelmed by events on Capitol Hill or elsewhere.

Several examples of failure to observe these principles can be found in the record of the Truman Administration. Certainly one of the most important events of that administration was the formulation of the European Recovery Program, but that great event did not get the newspaper display it deserved. It was announced, after many months of preparation, by Secretary of State George Marshall in a speech at Harvard University, but on the same day President Truman called a press conference and issued two statements, now comparatively unimportant, which blanketed the European recovery announcement.

Similarly the executive branch of the government sometimes fails to recognize that even modern communications can accommodate only so much material in any given day. The last day before Congress rises for a recess is always a busy time when the press associations' wires and the radio news bulletins are occupied with the final rush of legislation. Neglecting this fact the State Department just before the Christmas recess of 1947 released all the material in support of its European Recovery Program—a document running to nearly 150 pages. As a result, this extremely important document was never reported adequately in most of the newspapers of the country.

Some attempts have been made in the past to avoid this kind of conflict. During the war, for example, an effort was made to clear speeches by various agency and department heads so that they did not compete with one another for public attention nor contain conflicting statements, nor disclose information of strategic importance. After the war, Charles Ross, President Truman's press secretary, attempted to time important news releases so as to avoid conflict, and Cabinet officers often cleared their foreign policy speeches with the Department of State, but in peacetime, these procedures have seldom been subject to an orderly routine.

4. *The Tough Task of Coordination*

The President must contrive to coordinate the various departments of the executive branch so that one Cabinet officer is not publicly contradicting another Cabinet officer nor the President himself. President Truman achieved this cooperation to a large extent during the formulation of the European Recovery Program and Congressional action on it. But in 1948 he did not achieve cooperation on the Palestine question; on this issue the Secretaries of State and Defense were sometimes supporting different policies and at times even differing with the White House itself in public statements. The President must persuade his Cabinet officers to accept his policies or else force them to resign. For if he does not, Cabinet officers will be differing privately and before long their private quarrels will get into public discussion, creating a sense of division and disunity in the government.

In recent years there have been many instances of lack of coordination among the executive departments. For example, when President Truman, after the end of the second World War, decided on a stern policy of opposition to Soviet expansion, his Secretary of Commerce, Henry Wallace, raised certain objections which were not carefully thrashed out in Cabinet meetings. As a result, the President and Mr. Wallace gradually drifted further and further apart until the latter was finally forced to resign.

Again, in the late Spring of 1948, the United States decided to grant *de facto* recognition of the state of Israel. This was done in such a way, however, that neither the President nor the State Department had time to inform our ambassadors at the United Nations or in the European capitals. Similarly, about at the same time, the United States sent a long note through General Bedell Smith, its ambassador in Moscow, to the Soviet Government outlining U. S. foreign policy and ending with an indication that the U. S. Government might be willing to enter into diplomatic negotiations on a number of issues that had divided Washington and Moscow. No word of this, however, was passed along to the American ambassadors in Paris or London. Hence, for several days public opinion at home and abroad was confused about the real intentions of U. S. policy.

A third example came during the heat of the 1948 Presidential campaign. President Truman embarrassed his own Secretary of State by proposing to send, under secret and dramatic circumstances, Chief Justice Fred M. Vinson as a special envoy to Moscow to attempt a bilateral settlement of the German question. Coming as a complete surprise to Secretary Marshall and Under-Secretary Lovett, those officials protested so vigorously that the President hastily called off the scheme.

Obviously, incidents such as these create in the minds of Europeans doubt as to the stability of American policy and therefore tend to weaken American prestige. They also confuse and divide American public opinion and make it difficult to mobilize substantial public support for a policy which has been thus badly handled.

5. *Is the President's Power Dangerous?*

In conclusion, there is a tangential consideration growing out of the President's influence over public opinion that is of extreme importance. It is this: The power of the President in the realm of public opinion is now so great that, if it were abused, it might threaten our democratic institutions.

The Number One Voice

Consider what could happen, for example, if an eloquent and personable President with a well-organized staff really concentrated on the task of swaying public opinion in favor of his policies. Instead of coming into his press conference and saying that he had nothing to announce, he would be prepared to release whatever he liked, and the fact of his announcing it would make it news. Instead of holding his press conferences twice a week, as Franklin Roosevelt did, or once a week as Truman does, he could hold them every day if he chose. Instead of ignoring most of the arguments made against his policies, he could answer these directly or have his Cabinet participate much more than it now does in the debates on measures on Capitol Hill. Instead of making periodic checks on public opinion when crises arise, he could have much more careful checks made continuously. He could use the radio much oftener than at present to inform and persuade the voters.

The question, therefore, is no longer whether the President has sufficient power to balance the legislature in the constant battle for the mind of the people. The past advantage of the Congress has been redressed by modern communications. The question now is: How will the President use his great, new, extra-constitutional powers? Will he use them effectively and wisely in order to give the people strong leadership along the paths of democracy and international cooperation, or will he yield to the temptation to abuse them, and his constitutional powers, for his own glorification and to the detriment of our delicately balanced system of government?

The danger of the latter development in the foreseeable future seems remote. In any case the great safeguard against any such threat is an informed public opinion.

CHAPTER FOUR

THE MIRROR CALLED CONGRESS

By Cabell Phillips

THE CONGRESS of the United States speaks with many tongues, not always intelligibly and often confusedly. But its collective voice thunders into every cranny of our national existence, stirring thought, evoking controversy, shaping the attitudes and convictions of 148 million people.

As the legislative branch of the government, the Congress exerts tremendous influence on our foreign policy. It exerts this influence in three ways:

First, through its debates, Congress plays an outstanding role in influencing the decision on any big issue before the country.

Second, through the close contacts between members of Congress and their constituents, Congress mirrors the public opinion that it has helped to form. Congress is reluctant to pass any bill unless its members are certain it has solid, grass-roots support.

Third, through control of the purse strings and through its general authority, and the practices of the legislative process, Congress wields direct influence over the executive branch of the government.

All these factors tend to make the power of the Congress approximately co-equal with that of the Executive in the field of foreign affairs. The division of authority can be stated in this way:

The formulation of foreign policy is the function of the executive branch of the government. It is the job of the

President, assisted by the State Department; he alone is authorized by the Constitution to negotiate with other governments. But the implementation of foreign policy, through the ratification of treaties, the enactment of enabling legislation and, most important of all, through the appropriation of funds, is the function of the Congress.

1. How Congress Functions in Foreign Policy

Historically the two principal Congressional bodies dealing with foreign policy have been the Senate Committee on Foreign Relations and the House Committee on Foreign Affairs. In years past, the upper house has asserted leadership, its assent being necessary for the ratification of treaties and for the confirmation of ambassadors. Traditionally, the lower house has been distinctly a junior partner in the business of foreign affairs.

The increasing emphasis upon the dollar as an instrument of foreign policy has given the House of Representatives a new importance in foreign affairs, for dollars cannot be spent for any purpose without the assent of the House. "Dollar diplomacy," in fact, is again used by critics to describe our foreign policy. The Russians have so labeled it throughout Western Europe, and Henry Wallace made the phrase a shibboleth in his Progressive Party crusade. But whether or not we have "dollar diplomacy" today in the traditional and invidious sense, we do have a diplomacy in which dollars are an essential factor.

The trend began with the Lend-lease program which set a pattern of direct economic assistance to foreign powers for the accomplishment of mutually beneficial aims. The emphasis in our spending program shifted from military to economic objectives soon after the close of World War II, with the $3,750,000,000 loan to Britain, the Greek-Turkish Aid Program and, finally, the Marshall Plan. The figures are startling. The 1948-49 appropriations for the implementation of American foreign policy, including the expenses of our Defense Department, amounted to almost $23 billion. Ten years ago, in the fiscal year 1938-39, the sum of the appropriation for this purpose was slightly over $2 billion.[1]

In consequence of these increased expenditures, Congress, and more particularly the House Appropriations Committee, wields a new power in foreign relations. It controls the purse strings and hence is in a position to determine whether or not a given program of foreign aid will be carried out at all, as well as the scope and pattern of the operation.

In the closing weeks of the Eightieth Congress (June 1948) the fate of the Marshall Plan rested precariously in the hands of Representative John Taber, a New York Republican with a fanatical and single-minded devotion to economy in the disposition of public monies. As Chairman of the Appropriations Committee, Mr. Taber insisted upon elaborate and protracted hearings on all aspects of ERP, resolutely covering all the ground that other committees of two houses had previously explored. At the end, his Committee brought out a report reducing ERP funds by almost 25 percent from the amount previously authorized in the enabling legislation and already approved by the Senate. He and his committeemen were deaf to the almost frantic appeals, not only of Secretary Marshall and ECA Administrator Hoffman, but of Senator Vandenberg and other Republican supporters of the bipartisan aid program. Taber insisted that his committee had better and more recent in-

[1] These are the figures:

	1948-49	1938-39
	(millions of dollars)	
U. S. Department of State	$ 202.7	$ 16.6
Army, Navy, Air Forces	13,714.8	2,057.6
Administration costs in occupied areas	1,300.0	—
Economic Cooperation Administration (Marshall Plan)	4,000.0	—
Other foreign aid programs	730.7	—
Payment on quota due to International Monetary Fund	2,062.5	—
Payment on quota due to International Bank	635.0	—
Total	$22,645.7	$2,074.2

formation on the extent of need in Europe than the earlier committees, and that the curtailed sum would meet those needs. His argument won a surprising victory; the curtailed appropriation passed the House by a large majority.[2]

This heedless and arbitrary action by the House of Representatives occasioned widespread alarm. Anne O'Hare McCormick wrote:

> The House of Representatives has done more to undermine the Marshall Plan than the Cominform, revived for that purpose, has been able to do in an all-out campaign of sabotage, and the Communists are naturally exultant.[3]

The damage was largely repaired after a bitter fight in conference between the Senate and House Appropriations Committees. But the House had made a show of new and surprising strength in its purse-string control of foreign policy.

The possibility that the Senate will reject a treaty, or that the House will emasculate an important appropriation bill, means that the framers of foreign policy, the President and the State Department, as they shape new proposals, are much concerned with Congressional attitudes. Few blunders are more damaging to American prestige abroad than to have a new phase of foreign policy announced from the White House, only to have it negated later by a balky Congress. The greatest source of overseas skepticism regarding United States policy is this division of authority. Our friends abroad are obsessed with the fear that the Congress may reverse or upset Presidential programs which depend for their success upon continuity of purpose and operation.

2. How Congress Affects Opinion on Foreign Policy

Congress plays a tremendous role in the moulding of public opinion. In the realm of national affairs and foreign

---
[2] No record was made of the votes. This is perhaps an indication of sensitivity to public opinion.
[3] *New York Times,* June 7, 1948.

policy its public opinion potential is almost as great as that of the President. For where the President speaks once or twice on an issue, by voice or through the instrument of a state paper, the voice of Congress may reverberate for many days or weeks on the same issue. The President, because of his exalted position, may achieve greater immediate impact. But the repetitive effect of Congressional debate will frequently attain deeper penetration into people's minds.

This is even more true with respect to foreign policy than to domestic policy. Because foreign affairs is a remote and esoteric concept to the general run of people, their natural tendency is to "leave it to the experts" and to base their opinions, if any, on whatever expert's views are most readily available or seem most plausible.

For a great many people—probably for the great majority beyond the area of influence of the big metropolitan newspapers—the local Congressman or Senator is the expert on foreign affairs. He is on the scene in Washington where such great issues are concocted. He may have made a speech on the subject or taken part in committee deliberations. He may even have gone to some remote corner of the globe to study the situation at first hand. His vote may have had a decisive bearing on the whole shape and purpose of a given policy. In any event, he has been assiduous in informing his constituents of what he is thinking or doing about the matter. For those who want an opinion, and cannot or will not assume "the intolerable labor of thought" to arrive at one themselves, he supplies one ready-made for instant use.

Moreover, floor debate in Congress and committee hearings dramatize complex issues and synthesize them for public consumption. Angry, intemperate statements are made which, even though not bearing directly on the problem at hand, invest it with drama and excitement. The question is lifted out of its naturally drab and academic environment to become a front-page controversy.

Thus, Congress is the nation's most popular forum and its greatest sounding board. Congressmen's words—foolish as well as wise, prejudiced as well as reasoned—are carried to every hamlet and crossroads in the country. The deliberations of Congress are followed by the greatest concentration of news and radio reporters anywhere in the world. The Washington press corps numbers about 1,100. An average day's "file" by the three leading press associations on Congressional news alone will run anywhere from 25,000 to 30,000 words. Individual correspondents probably boost this total another 15,000 to 20,000. Nearly all members of Congress, moreover, supply their constituents more or less regularly with written or spoken transcripts of their views. Many members mail weekly mimeographed news letters to long lists of newspapers and voters in their districts. According to a recent count, 140 members of the House and Senate make regular weekly radio platters in a studio built for the purpose on the top floor of the new House office building. Mailed to radio stations back home, the platters are then broadcast as regular sustaining features and have a direct effect on public opinion.

In these publicity efforts, the Congressman probably is not aiming so much at influencing the voters' thinking on the major issues of the day as at obtaining public approval of his own votes and speeches. His purpose is to insure understanding and approval by his constituents of the manner in which he has discharged his Congressional duties, so that they will be persuaded to keep him in office. But an inescapable by-product is the moulding of public attitudes for or against the proposals upon which the member reports.

3. *How Does the Congress Make Up Its Mind?*

If the Congress wields such decisive influence on foreign policy and in the formation of public opinion, it becomes important to know the answers to questions such as these: How does Congress make up its mind? How well informed is the average member when he casts a vote on some vital issue of foreign policy?

Probably the most consistent note to be found in the autobiographical writings of men who have served in the national legislature is the inexorable pressure of time. The conscientious member is so overwhelmed with the volume and diversity of his duties that he finds himself in a continuous race with the clock. Congressmen all complain that they seldom have opportunity to familiarize themselves with more than a fraction of the legislation on which they have to vote. Jerry Voorhis, who represented a California district for ten years prior to 1946, writes:

> Congressmen are supposed to pass good laws for the government of the United States. Compared to that duty and obligation, all the other things Congressmen do are of almost insignificant consequence.
>
> But had I never written a single letter, or done a single worthwhile service for a constituent, or consulted a single department, or attended a single meeting, conference or lecture during my whole congressional career, even then I could barely have done a completely effective legislative job on the number of bills in which I believed it my clear duty to take an active interest.[4]

And George Galloway, in his exhaustive study of Congress and its mounting responsibilities, concludes that "Representative government in the United States can be saved only by wise and deliberate curtailment of the business of Congress."[5]

To understand Congressional attitudes on foreign affairs we have to ask just what is the member trying to represent, the nation or his particular constituency? Is he ruled by his personal convictions as to what is best for the national welfare, or by the expediencies of the next election? The answer is pretty obvious. Complete integrity of purpose and action is probably a more expensive luxury in politics than i

[4] In his book, *Confessions of a Congressman,* New York, Doubleday, 1947, p. 302.
[5] *Congress at the Crossroads,* New York, Crowell, 1946, p. 83.

any other gainful pursuit a man can follow. Senators and Representatives are not elected by the nation at large. They are elected by a majority of the voters of their particular states, or districts. To remain in public life they have to satisfy the *mores*, the aspirations, the whims and the prejudices of that majority. The voters in many constituencies throughout the country, it is true, show only a limited interest in foreign affairs; for them foreign policy is a remote, unintelligible abstraction. Members from such districts are seldom under pressure from their constituents to take a stand one way or the other. On the other hand, because of their freedom from home pressure, they are perhaps more susceptible to influence from other pressure groups with axes to grind.

Congress as a whole, it is safe to say, resembles more a mirror, reflecting the sentiments already formed in the country, than a beacon, guiding public opinion along new paths and to new conclusions.

Admitting the basic considerations of self-interest, what is the process by which a Congressman makes a decision on a specific issue? First in importance is party policy, the party line. On every major issue the policy committee of each party determines in advance of debate, often in advance of the committee vote, what the party's attitude toward the particular bill is to be. This is seldom a completely democratic process, participated in by a majority of the party members, but rather the decision of a handful of leaders. Sometimes such decisions are difficult or impossible to reach because of fundamental splits within the leadership itself. Thus, on the first ECA appropriation, there was wide division between the Vandenberg forces on the one hand and the economy group represented by Senator Taft and Representative Taber. No hard Republican line emerged. As a rule, however, the policy committees do reach a decision for or against, or to modify, each major legislative proposal. This decision is passed down the line, orally and informally, through the party whips to the members. There is no stern obligation on the individual member to accept the party line. But among Congressmen, party loyalty is a worthwhile virtue and, lacking compelling reasons to follow a different course, most members vote as they are told.

Next in importance are the committee reports. Most members find time to scan these documents hurriedly to get a general impression of what the bill in question is about. If one of the committee members happens to be a close friend, or someone whom he particularly admires, the Congressman will probably, other things being equal, follow that person's lead. He seldom studies the text of a bill unless it is short, or unless he feels the need to get his name in the *Congressional Record* by a little oratorical exercise. In that case he may scan the bill for some peg on which to base an objection or to raise a question.

Another source of information is the general comment which the member picks up in his daily newspaper reading and in personal contacts. Like less privileged citizens, he is much influenced by the views of his favorite columnist or commentator; he reads the public opinion polls; he listens also to the trend of cloakroom and office discussion. Members of Congress are avid newspaper readers. In addition to the more important papers from their home states, nearly all of them scan at least one Washington and one New York paper daily. If consideration of a bill is protracted and is much in the news, the Senator or Representative will often have reached a reasonably firm conclusion as to how he will stand before the issue comes to a vote.

Least important of the factors influencing the average Congressman's mind is floor debate. It is seldom indeed that the tide on a bill has been turned by the force of oratory. Speeches are for public, not Congressional, consumption; most members use the time thus afforded to go to lunch, visit the barber shop, catch up on their office work or prepare the draft of a speech of their own.

In the final analysis it is the sentiment back home that determines how members will vote on most issues. All members of Congress receive a great deal of mail, from a few hundred to as many as a thousand letters daily. Many letters ask favors, but many also convey local attitudes and points of view. Most members use one or two key persons in each community as their points of contact, both for political maneuvers and to gauge local opinion. On controversial issues these strategically placed observers report what the voters are thinking. Carrying this idea further, some enterprising members have adapted public opinion polling to their own use. They mail questionnaires on certain issues to cross sections of local voting lists, asking constituents to mark their preference as between two or more alternative courses of action. Representative Robert J. Corbett, Republican, of Pennsylvania, has followed this practice for several years, receiving as many as 8,000 answers to a single questionnaire. Commenting upon the value of such sampling, particularly as a means of cross-checking large volumes of unsolicited advice, he reported to the House:

> Obviously many of the pictures of public opinion on given issues which I had believed to be true were found to be very false. I had been judging opinion on the basis of unsolicited letters and telephone calls from constituents. Like many others I tended to believe on a majority of questions that those who wrote, wired or telephoned reflected typical opinion. They simply did not do so in most cases. Rather, they generally represented vocal minorities. Organized pressure groups and individuals have long since learned all the tricks on how to give Members of Congress a false picture of public sentiment. There is one easy corrective—solicit opinion on a scale large enough to eliminate the possibility of error.[6]

All this is, to a degree at least, an indictment of Congress in that Congressmen put too much emphasis on their role as mirrors of public opinion, not enough on their role as moulders of public opinion. It is also an indictment of the American people. For obviously if we had a better informed

[6] *Congressional Record,* March 15, 1946, v. 92, pt. 10, p. 1400.

public opinion Congress would be under greater pressure to consider legislation on its intrinsic merit.

4. The Congress and the Executive

The relations between Congress and the Executive Department—particularly the Presidency and the State Department—are a vital factor in any discussion of public opinion and foreign policy. When these relations are friendly and cordial the task of informing the public and of framing policy is greatly simplified. But when there are protracted misunderstandings and outright antagonisms, the effect is to confuse the public mind.

There should be a two-way flow of information between the executive and legislative branches. The State Department should give to the Congress, as fully as possible, information that the members of Congress, in turn, would pass on to their constituents. The Department should get from the Congress some indication of what the nation is thinking.

Poor relations cut off this two-way flow of information. Policy becomes mired in partisan politics and personal animosities. Often the citizen is asked to choose between two diametrically opposed views of policy—one the Executive's and the other Congress'. Finally, and most important, poor relations deprive the Executive and the State Department of the kind of Congressional support that they have needed and will need increasingly in the future.

Unfortunately the relations between the Congress and the Executive have too often been unfriendly. One of the most persistent areas of conflict between the executive and legislative branches of the federal government has been the control of foreign affairs. The delegation of powers by the Constitution is not specific and in many places appears to permit a confusing overlapping. While the Constitution gives to the Congress the right to declare war, it gives to the President and the Senate the right to make peace treaties. And it is silent on such subjects as neutrality, abrogation of treaties and the recognition of new governments. Presidents Washington, Lincoln, McKinley and Wilson all fell into violent controversies with Congress over the control of foreign policy, and over great periods of our national history the initiative has shifted from one branch to the other. Following a long period of Senate domination stemming from the reaction to Wilsonian diplomacy and the defeat of the Versailles Treaty, Franklin D. Roosevelt reasserted the Presidential prerogative and retained it until his death. With the end of World War II and the emphasis upon economic aid as an instrument of foreign policy, Congress re-emerged as an almost co-equal power with the Executive. That this development was not accompanied by the acrimony and stalemating which have marked previous resurgences can be attributed to the success of the bipartisan foreign policy in the foreign aid programs of 1947 and 1948.

In the evolution of the Marshall Plan, President Truman sought and received the cooperation of many strong Republican leaders in Congress such as Senator Vandenberg and Representative Christian Herter. Similarly, our representation in the United Nations and our general program there have been chiefly the products of cooperation. On the other hand, the President has not cooperated as fully as he might either with the opposition or with Congress as a whole on problems relating to Germany, Palestine and the Far East. The inclusion of the China Aid Program as a part of the Marshall Plan was, as much as anything else, a disciplinary gesture by the Republican-controlled Congress to show the President and the people that it, too, had an important say in foreign affairs.

On the whole the relations between the Congress and the President in the field of foreign policy have been more harmonious in recent years than they were in the past. But the same cannot be said for the relations between the Congress and the State Department.

Since 1944 the growth of bipartisanship in foreign policy

has brought about close working relations between members of the Senate Foreign Relations Committee, particularly Senators Connally and Vandenberg, and the Secretary of State. But despite all these efforts at understanding and good will, there is still a large gap to be filled before a harmonious relationship between Congress and the Department is established. Had there been a full measure of mutual confidence Congress would hardly have written into the legislation creating ECA provisions designed to eliminate participation by the State Department in the administration of the Foreign Aid Program. In the long series of hearings that preceded enactment of the program, as well as in other encounters, mutual hostility, suspicion and resentment were displayed by both legislators and administrators.

Many Congressmen harbor an unreasoning prejudice against foreign service officers and State Department officials. In part, this is a traditional attitude which has no logical basis today. The average Congressman cherishes in his mind a sort of caricature of himself as a rough, hardheaded, practical politician. In sharp contrast is his mental picture of the diplomat as a clever, effete dandy. Probably no member of the Eightieth Congress would publicly confess these illusions, but there can be no doubt they exist subconsciously, and it is certain that they color the attitudes of many legislators on questions of foreign policy. Prejudice and hostility are intensified when the language and problems of modern diplomacy prove too complex for the unprepared Congressional mind to grasp.

A second cause of antagonism toward the State Department is the distrust that many Americans, members of Congress included, instinctively feel for foreigners and foreign affairs, generally. This distrust, a reflection of the attitudes of their constituents,[7] is extended to government officials concerned with international relations.

The third cause is more substantial than either of the

[7] See the discussion by Dr. Kriesberg on pp. 57-58.

foregoing and, hence, is more amenable to correction. Congress feels that the State Department is derelict in not supplying all the information needed to legislate intelligently on foreign affairs. It has not been unusual for State Department officials to decline to discuss the details of delicate diplomatic negotiations on the ground that premature disclosure of the facts would endanger international agreement. Moreover they know that confidential information laid before Congressional committees, even in executive session, has frequently "leaked" to favored columnists and commentators. These leaks at times have seriously embarrassed the State Department, even causing minor crises in our foreign relations.

In the Summer of 1947, when the Herter Committee of the House was preparing to go overseas for its memorable study of European recovery prospects, it requested and received from the State Department a highly confidential dossier on a score or more of foreign government officials with whom the committee wanted to confer. These memoranda contained some very candid, and not always flattering, appraisals of individuals then—and now—in high places. It obviously was material for the eyes of the committee members alone, about as top secret as any document well could be. But within a matter of hours after the group embarked at New York, a local newspaper ran large excerpts from the dossier which a member of the committee had leaked to it. The most earnest apologies and explanations of the State Department did not suffice to soothe the outraged sensibilities of some of the dignitaries who had been most acutely "profiled."

Newspapermen, for professional reasons, are conscientious in respecting off-the-record confidences. They are understandably embittered, therefore, when an important story which they have been sitting on for days or weeks suddenly breaks from an unexpected quarter. During 1947 a particularly noteworthy agreement was negotiated with a certain Balkan power. Shortly before the highly secret arrangements were concluded, the Secretary of State gave an off-the-record preview of the situation to a select group of Senators and Representatives. Later, he gave a similar background explanation to a picked group of correspondents, also off the record. The formal announcement was to come three days later at 6 P.M. On the morning of the release date, the late editions of a New York paper carried a full and accurate résumé of the agreement.

No great diplomatic injury resulted, fortunately, but a score of outraged correspondents stormed into the office of the abashed Secretary to know why they, who had assiduously guarded his confidence, had thus been scooped by a newspaperman who had not even attended the secret seminar. The answer soon became apparent. The enterprising reporter (who had not even known about the off-the-record press conference) had been furnished just enough tips by a Congressional friend to enable him to extract the full story from another acquaintance on Capitol Hill.

But if such experiences seem to justify the Department in a "closed mouth" policy, it must be admitted, on the other hand, that a Congressional committee called upon to legislate on vital matters of foreign policy cannot operate effectively in a partial vacuum of information.

There is an awareness in the Department of the necessity of improving its relations with Congress, and it tries conscientiously to better them. It tries to supply advice that is necessary on bills and resolutions under consideration in Congress, and it sends Department heads and experts to Congressional committees to state their views on particular policies. Moreover, there are an increasing number of occasions when leading members of the Department and the Congress assemble informally and unofficially to explore foreign policy and to try to reach agreement on steps to be taken. Again, the Department builds up good will by running errands and doing favors for Congressmen. For example, it helps their constituents get passports and visas, it gives assistance in answering questions, and it makes its services available in preparing technical speeches or reports.

But the contributions toward more cooperative relations by both Congress and the Executive are still far short of what is needed. There is much that both branches can and must do to improve the situation. Obviously the improvement must be made if our policies are to have broadly based support among the nation's citizenry. One cannot expect the businessman, the farmer or the mechanic to think clearly on national issues that have become obscured in the smoke of intra-governmental rivalry.

5. *An Informed Congress, An Informed Public*

How can Congress achieve a better discharge of its functions in the field of foreign affairs? And especially how can it help in the task of achieving a better informed public opinion?

Of prime importance is an effort by Congress to inform itself more effectively. Some of the machinery toward that end is already at hand.

Under the Reorganization Act of 1947, each of the two legislative committees on foreign policy acquired a four-man professional staff. These are ably manned at present. They have, moreover, recourse to the Legislative Reference Service of the Library of Congress, which has also been expanded and improved. The relations between these staffs and the Congressional liaison section of the State Department are excellent. There are, apparently, no serious bottlenecks in the transmission of technical information between the Department and the committees of Congress.

But there is no organized and consistent effort to inform Congress as a whole on matters of foreign policy. Formal committee reports, related to specific matters of legislation, are about the only educational efforts undertaken by these committees.

It is recommended that the two committees, either jointly or separately, undertake the job of keeping their respective houses regularly abreast of foreign policy matters through the frequent publication of interim reports or bulletins.

One proposal is that the two committees merge into a joint Senate-House Committee on Foreign Affairs. This plan, however, has serious drawbacks. For one reason, a 38-man committee (assuming that the two present committees would simply combine) would be unwieldy. For another, there would be difficulty in overcoming the deeply imbedded prerogatives and prejudices in which each group is now steeped. Neither wishes to yield to the other in any matter of authority and prestige. Finally, under the Constitution certain functions are delegated exclusively to one group or the other, rendering joint action legally doubtful. Only a Constitutional amendment would take care of this difficulty.

However, there are no barriers to the establishment of a quasi-official group, representative not only of the Foreign Affairs and Foreign Relations Committees, but also of committees concerned with appropriations and the armed services. Such a group could maintain constant liaison at the policy-making level with the White House, State Department and National Defense Establishment. It would participate, in an advisory capacity, with the Executive on policy making and keep the Congress informed both on new policy formation and on execution. By including the three main constituent aspects of foreign policy—legislative, military and financial—it could bring all three into focus simultaneously. If the requisite prestige and authority could be conferred upon such a group, its influence would be tremendous. Programs could be worked out with an eye both to their effectiveness in international relations and their acceptability to Congress and the people.

Besides the need for informing itself, Congress should recognize the obligation of government to inform its citizens of policies and programs that intimately affect their daily lives. It should abandon its purely negative and repressive attitude toward informational activities, adopting instead an affirmative tone. It should insist that the public be given all the information it needs to form intelligent opinions. It should set up high standards of adequacy and objectivity for the presentation of information, and high qualifications in the persons engaged in all federal publicity operations. These operations need not impinge upon the prerogatives of the press nor descend to partisan propaganda.

This need is recognized by students of government inside and outside of Congress. Nevertheless, Congress has shown itself on numerous occasions unwilling to delegate to the Executive much latitude in the field of opinion formation. Almost every outstanding informational and educational program proposed by federal agencies in the last decade has encountered bitter enmity in Congress. Unquestionably, some of these programs have been badly planned, as the record of some of the more ambitious New Deal agencies has shown. On the other hand, it is the sheerest folly to expect a government agency to make its problems known and understood by the public without intelligent and repeated explanation. This is particularly true of foreign policy.[8]

Moreover, by conducting its own affairs in a more enlightened manner, Congress itself can play an important part in enlightening public opinion. Few activities of Congress are as effective in informing large segments of the population as committee hearings and investigations. Such investigations in the past as the Black Committee on lobbying, the LaFollette Committee on civil liberties, the Truman-Mead Committee on war frauds, and even the House Committee on un-American Activities, have had tremendous effects on public opinion. If these Congressional investigations could be broadened and lifted out of the category of persecutions or

---

[8] See Chapter One, pp. 37-40.

witch hunts, they might become educational laboratories where broad agreements on national policy could be synthesized out of many divergent views.

Finally, Congress must recognize its duty to lead public opinion. This duty has not been recognized in the past, and is not recognized today. On the contrary, there is a great deal of evidence to show that Congress is behind, not ahead, of public opinion on most matters of major policy. On such current questions as housing, public health, aid to education and universal military training, nearly every recent test has indicated a heavy preponderance of popular sentiment favoring action. Yet Congress either has not acted at all on these measures or has acted tardily and reluctantly. There is no more dearly held axiom in our political folklore than "He who sticks his neck out pulls back a nub."

But quite apart from considerations of self-preservation, most members honestly believe that their proper function is to be guided by public opinion as it already exists among their constituents, rather than to lead it into new paths. Many take this attitude because, being realists, they recognize their own limitations. They believe that only a few men of exceptional character and ability, whose constituents are tolerant and enlightened, can work successfully at moulding public opinion. For measurable progress in this direction, we shall have to have a greater proportion of Representatives and Senators with qualities of true statesmanship.

CHAPTER FIVE

WHEN THE BIG GUNS SPEAK [1]

By Hanson W. Baldwin

TIME WAS when the American military had little influence upon American foreign policy; in past generations, the civilian leaders of government formed foreign policy and the military leaders framed a military policy adequate to support that foreign policy. The military policy, however, was approved (or, more usually, emasculated) by Congress. But today the military help to frame foreign policy and to influence public opinion in peace as in war.

1. The Importance of Military Opinion

"Our God and soldier we alike adore,
 When at the brink of ruin, not before;
 After deliverance, both alike requited,
 Our God forgotten, and our soldiers slighted."

So wrote Francis Quarles in 1635 of the public's vacillating attitude toward the soldier.

This cyclical variation in public opinion long has been characteristic of democracies. The soldier has been extolled in war, forgotten in peace. His opinions, heeded with respect in the midst of trial, are ignored in the ease of security.

Until World War II, the United States followed this traditional pattern. A nation thoroughly republican in its sympathies, a nation immune to serious attack behind the ram-

[1] Some of the material on which this chapter is based was gathered by Avery Leiserson, Assistant Professor of Political Science, University of Chicago.

parts of the seas, we tended to slight our fighting men and to deride their opinions as "nationalistic" or "inflammatory" until the hour of need. We found no requirement in peacetime for sizable military establishments; our geography, our environment and our psychology all conditioned us against maintenance of large standing forces. Until World War II the average American knew little about the services; even the uniforms were strange and unusual. Twenty-odd years ago when the author of this chapter was in the Navy as midshipman and officer, his uniform was mistaken often for that of a railroad gateman, a bus conductor or a messenger boy.

The peacetime United States of the nineteenth and twentieth centuries, like the England of Francis Quarles, displayed a faint and, for those days, a healthy skepticism of military might; we were influenced but slightly by the military viewpoint.

But all this has changed. The atomic bomb, radioactive dusts, biological agents, deadly gases, long-range planes, new types of submarines and supersonic missiles have destroyed America's insular security. Terrain barriers, icy wastes and leagues of ocean have vanished in the foreshortened geography of the air age. Since Hiroshima, our nation has been exposed to potential attack, attack so devastating in its potentialities, so sudden and swift that an unprecedented emphasis has been placed in peacetime upon security, military security. No longer will it suffice to raise fighting forces after war starts. Today, the emphasis must be upon readiness potential rather than upon mobilization potential; large military forces must be maintained in peacetime.

We have but recently emerged from the Valley of the Shadow. We have breathed the heady air of conquest; we have seen our flag everywhere triumphant, our enemies prostrate. One cannot easily in a few months of history forget the high moments of yesterday, nor is it possible to turn at

When the Big Guns Speak

once—after a war so vast and so "total" as World War II —to other forces, other figures, other men than those who led us to victory. The United States was blessed in World War II with exceptional military leaders, men who made their mark on history and carved their place in the American heart. The abilities of these men, the Marshalls, the Bradleys, the Eisenhowers, so marked in war, have been, in many instances, utilized in peacetime in semi-military or non-military pursuits. The wartime prestige of our military leaders and military services has carried over into this immediate post-war period and in some cases has been extended to non-military fields. The prestige of victory, and the outstanding ability of some of the military leaders, both help to explain why military opinion now is given such weight by the public.

We are still in an era of non-peace; we have left the "shooting war" behind, but the world is plainly "two worlds." The tension and strain of the existing international situation, and the aggressive, expansionist policies of Russia, have focused the thoughts of many Americans upon the possibility of another "shooting war" and have emphasized the importance of military opinion. Moreover, the very size and universality of the military establishment considered necessary in this age of atomic armaments and international tension tend to extend the influence of military opinion; each of us, for instance, knows one or more youngsters in the armed services; all of us wonder if our own sons and daughters must serve.

The fact of military influence upon public opinion is well established; that influence is undeniably greater today than in any prior peacetime period. And, whether we like this fact or not, there are compelling reasons for the military viewpoint's important part in formulating national opinion.

1. The military are charged with the *physical* security of the nation. Our military strength must be capable both

of backing up our political and moral commitments overseas and of protecting our vital economic interests. We must be careful, unless we want to court disaster, that our foreign policy commitments do not exceed our physical (military) ability to implement those commitments. Political policy, plus economic policy, plus psychological policy, plus military policy equal foreign policy; there is no equation if one of the factors is missing.

2. The military viewpoint is usually (though not always) the viewpoint of the pragmatist. The G-2, or intelligence, approach must be unemotional, logical, precise. Americans are notoriously wishful thinkers; their idealism always has required tempering with realism. The clinical approach of the military to international problems is a desirable element in the formulation of national policy.

3. Military security can no longer be measured solely in terms of armed men or conventional battlefields; the citizen is the soldier, the home front a campaign ground. Military security today means more than armies, navies and air forces; it connotes research laboratories, developmental proving grounds and wind tunnels, a world-wide intelligence system, an economic mobilization system, a civilian defense organization, in short a vast network of interlocking and mutually supporting agencies. To provide a reasonable degree of national security in the age of the atomic bomb and total war, the military must branch out into the fields of scientific research, industry, manpower, politico-military affairs and into nearly all the endeavors of man. The voice of the military must have a place in the councils of the nation; the body politic must give the military a hearing in the forum of public opinion, or there can be no hope of a sound defensive system.

The military viewpoint, therefore, not only is important in the formulation of public opinion in twentieth century America, but should be, and must be, important, if we are to survive as a nation.

2. The Military Viewpoint within Government

Among the vehicles for the interchange of information and opinion in Washington, the first, by virtue of rank, is the Cabinet. For making policy, however, this forum is less important in reality than in appearance; the military viewpoint, though it may be expressed at Cabinet meetings, is rarely expounded and clarified there. Discussions of policies may sometime be initiated at Cabinet meetings, but such discussions necessarily are brief, discursive, and usually abortive since the Cabinet suffers from the lack of a secretariat. Cabinet meetings serve principally to provide a sounding board for the President's ideas.

More important is the "kitchen cabinet" or the "little cabinet," the group of the close advisers which, in one form or another, every President gathers around him. This group usually has much to do with actual formulation of national policy, both domestic and foreign. The military viewpoint may, or may not, be represented, depending upon the personality and inclination of each President.

The Joint Chiefs of Staff also have direct access to the White House. The concern of this agency is with grand strategy, politico-military problems, and mobilizing the national strength for war.

The new National Security Council, headed by the President, and with the Secretaries of State, Defense, Army, Navy and Air and representatives of other agencies as members, is envisaged as the vehicle for the coordination of military and foreign policy. It may well become far more effective than the Cabinet in expressing and promoting the military viewpoint, particularly since it has the advantage of a permanent Secretariat and a formalized agenda. The Council has been criticized because of the predominance of the military members.

In the Atomic Energy Commission, all the commissioners are civilians, but Army, Navy and Air Force officers occupy important executive and administrative posts, and no less than three liaison committees or bodies—all of them with large or predominant military membership—keep in intimate touch with the Commission's program. Thus, indirectly, the armed services are assured a strong voice in the Commission's decisions. Under the law, if the Commission rules against these services, the military may appeal directly to the President; hence the Commission, though independent of the military in theory, is actually profoundly influenced by them.

The National War College, which brings together officers of the Army, Navy and Air Force and State Department or Foreign Service officers, is another institution which propagates the military viewpoint. The influence of the College is long term and educational; it is not an administrative body. It represents a hopeful and far-sighted attempt to relate power to policy and, also, to integrate foreign policy with military policy.

The Central Intelligence Agency has for its principal executives military, naval and air officers, either active, reserve or retired. The CIA's estimates of the world situation, based on both overt and covert sources, and of the impact abroad of American policies, are distributed throughout the key agencies of government and are placed on the President's desk. Obviously, these views of international affairs, seen primarily through military eyes, can have great influence in the formulation of foreign policy.

SANACC,[2] post-war successor to SWNCC, has been an important vehicle for the expression within government of service opinion, and for the formulation at lower levels of a coordinated military and foreign policy. The Assistant Secretaries of the State Department and of the Air Force, and the Under-Secretaries of the Army and Navy are members,

---

[2] The cryptic letters stand for State-Army-Navy-Air Coordinating Committee. SANACC is the present-day version of the pre-unification SWNCC or State-War-Navy Coordinating Committee.

but additional personnel from all these departments are also assigned to SANACC for full-time or part-time work. Liaison is at a level where the study of politico-military problems may be initiated—between the politico-military sections of the operations divisions of the staffs of the services and the pertinent geographical desk in the State Department. It is at these levels, for instance, that a study of the military and strategic consequences of our Palestine policy might be started. SANACC was a particularly useful instrument during the war, but, since the passage of the National Security Act of 1947, the new National Security Council has assumed many of SANACC's former functions and the Committee has become a sort of lower-level agency for the settlement of rather routine problems. Post-war occupation problems, once handled by SANACC, were transferred in 1948 to the joint responsibility of the Department of State and the Department of the Army. A slogan popular in the State Department in early 1948—"Snap back with SANACC!"—exemplifies with its faint suggestion of sarcasm the somewhat anomalous role of SANACC in the modern bureaucratic organization of Washington.

A civilian defense agency, as yet in embryo, may assume increasing importance as the atomic arms race continues, in the expression of the military viewpoint within and outside government. Decentralization, dispersion, evacuation, fire-fighting, etc., the numerous and baffling problems of cushioning atomic blows against our cities, would all be within the province of such an agency. Defense measures of this kind, which have a major effect upon our way of life, must and will be influenced by the military.

Such is the complex bureaucratic structure by which the military viewpoint is expressed within government. Policy is the product of a series of disagreements, hammered out on the anvil of inter-agency debate and discussion. During this process there is as much conflict among government agencies in the military and politico-military fields as in the economic or political field. But, once policy has been enunciated, the military agencies show more solidarity, particularly if that policy recognizes—as the Truman Doctrine does—the importance of military power. Because of its solidarity the military viewpoint has disproportionate strength when it conflicts with the views of the civilian agencies. In fact, in Washington today there is some potential danger that the military tail may wag the civilian dog.

The formidable catalogue given in previous paragraphs of governmental agencies that serve to incubate and express the military point of view should not be misinterpreted. Military opinion and military policy are never quite as formal, stylized and arranged as the catalogue suggests. There is no single, simplified and standardized process by which military opinion is expressed within government, but rather a multiplicity of means—some of them extravagantly regularized, others decidedly informal.

3. *The Military Viewpoint and the Public*

Under the National Security Act of 1947 the means and methods of interpreting the military point of view to the people are changing, as is the structure of the armed services. A unified public information service has been established in the Department of Defense, although each of the three armed services still retains its sizable, semi-autonomous publicity organization. The Secretary's office also includes in its growing personnel a number of officers whose sole function it is to deal at the top echelon with the broad policies of public relations, and to maintain close liaison with the public relations representatives of each service.

The growing importance of the Office of the Secretary of Defense in representing the military viewpoint is clear. In routine matters of information, the publicity of the armed services is decentralized and more or less autonomous, but matters involving major policies are cleared through the Secretary's office. Hence, there is now less room for *open* disagreement among the services than in the era preceding the passage of the unification act; the military viewpoint as presented to the public is more solidified than formerly. This is at once an advantage and a danger; it prevents the development among the services of divisive trends inimical to military efficiency, but it strengthens and may unduly emphasize the expression of an "official" military viewpoint to the public. Although it is still too early to draw hard and fast conclusions, one example may be cited as indicating the trend. The Secretary of Defense issued in early 1948 an order which forbade officers to discuss publicly, without prior approval of the Office of the Secretary of Defense, controversial policies or problems.

The Office of the Secretary of Defense, although not much concerned with the daily grist from the public relations mills of the three services, dispenses both information and opinion. It is not necessary, here, to enter into discussion of the Secretary's role, or the roles of his subordinates, the Secretaries of Army, Navy and Air Force. Whether or not these men represent the armed services or the American principle of civilian predominance over the military, whether they dominate, or are dominated by, the military viewpoint is clearly dependent upon their strength of character, their background, their abilities and convictions. In past years some Secretaries have been merely mouthpieces for the Army or the Navy. Others clearly have held the upper hand over the admirals and the generals. The best have been able to bridge the gap between civilian and military interests and attitudes. But no matter in what category a Secretary falls, at times, if he is to fulfill his function, he must present to the public the military point of view.

Such presentation is often accomplished by the Secretary of Defense, or the subordinate Secretaries, informally in interviews, at press conferences or at dinner parties; sometimes it is formalized in speeches or in statements to Congressional committees. Quite often—especially when a Secretary is adept in dealing with the press and the subject is delicate or controversial—the opinion he wishes to convey to the public may be sown like grain in the form of hints, in off-the-record, background, or not-for-attribution interviews. The trial balloon technique, a well-established Washington custom, has now been elevated to a higher art— the influencing of public opinion, and through it of policy, by anonymous interviews. The grain thus sown is reaped, of course, when the interviews or hints, quietly given, influence in favor of the military decisions pending in government, or modify decisions previously made but not in accordance with the military viewpoint.

Apart from the Secretary himself, who is the most important public relations representative of the National Military Establishment, there now exists in the Secretary's office an Office of Public Information with a civilian director. This director, an assistant to the Secretary, is responsible for "developing and coordinating over-all public information policy for the National Military Establishment" and guides and advises the Secretary of Defense on all public information matters. He has been vested by the Secretary with authority to make decisions in the Secretary's name. A common pressroom for all three services has been established in the Pentagon, which is now the official home of the Secretaries and Chiefs of Staff of the Army, Navy and Air Force. Thus, considerable progress has been made in canalizing all information about the National Military Establishment to the public through a common pipeline—a process which is undoubtedly helpful to inter-service unity, but which can unduly emphasize the voice of the military in Washington.

Below the secretarial level the machinery for disseminating military facts and approved military opinions is organized with all the thoroughness of a task force. Public information officers of the services have studied—with profit— the experience of the great corporations in dealing with the intangibles of public opinion, and they have been guided in setting up their organization and their policies by some of America's leading publicists, propagandists and advertising agencies. During and since the war, when the services first began to understand that public opinion was a weapon far more important than any individual item listed in their tables of equipment, the armed forces have included public information personnel as full-time specialists in their organizations.

The Army, the Navy and the Air Force all maintain large public information offices in Washington staffed with experts —many of them reserve officers formerly connected with privately owned information media—who specialize in contacts with the newspapers, radio, magazines, etc. The services maintain, also, a common school to which prospective public information officers are sent for "get-rich-quick," but nevertheless fairly inclusive, courses. The Navy has been holding periodic information seminars in Washington, addressed by experts, which are attended not only by PIO (public information officers) but also by the commanding officers of various activities.

The three information organizations head up in more or less parallel top echelons. The Army's public information chief, a lieutenant-general, heads a three-branched office of public information, Congressional relations, and troop information and education; he is answerable directly to the Chief of Staff. The Air Forces, since unification, have put their public relations under a civilian directly answerable to the Secretary of the Air Force. The Navy's Chief of Public Relations, a rear admiral, is also answerable to his Secretary. Each chief is also guided—at least theoretically—in policy or controversial questions by the Director of the Office of Public Information of the Secretary of Defense, who is now the top-level public relations representative of the military establishment. Each of these service chiefs or directors, who in rank are more or less on a policy-forming level in their respective departments, has under or associated with him a principal assistant of the rank of brigadier, major-general or colonel, or the equivalent, who has direct charge of the Department's day-by-day relationships with newspapers, the radio and other public information media.

These men have established in their Departments fairly elaborate offices which serve as clearing houses or channels for (and sometimes dams against) the flow of military information to the public. Public information officers attached to the various services, bureaus or subdivisions of their Departments funnel information to the main public information office where, usually after a lengthy process, press releases are composed. When the releases have been approved, sometimes by a multiplicity of offices, the information is made public.

The administrative decentralization of the public information system is carried even further; the Army, the Navy and the Air Force all maintain public information representatives with every major, and with many minor, commands. With respect to routine information about maneuvers, personnel, organization, etc., these organizations often ease the path of the press. They are particularly helpful in providing physical facilities, transportation, housing, mess, etc. But decentralization is more of a handicap than a help when information is wanted on army-wide, navy-wide, or air-force-wide issues, or on broad questions of policy.

Information offices sometimes have the habit, too, of turning mysteriously, like chameleons, into censorship offices when the story the reporter is trying to track down reflects discredit on the services. Too often, the best the reporter can expect then is a gilding of the facts, even if no positive handicaps are placed in his way. This, of course, is not a universal criticism. Many public information officers know that the best policy is frankness, and in fairness it should be said that the top echelons urge this policy on their subordinates. For example, Major-General Floyd Parks, formerly chief of the Army's Public Information Division, has said:

> Too many people in the armed forces have the idea that we can maintain good relations with the public by suppressing unsavory stories; by keeping them from being published and by taking counter measures designed to offset bad publicity. It is not possible to suppress news successfully, be it good or bad, and it's poor policy to try. The result generally is a distorted story that shows the matter in perspective out of all proportion to its actual importance. We must have complete frankness in our dealings with the public. A reputation for honesty is essential.

In addition to the formal mechanism for the dissemination of fact and opinion, many other devices are utilized by the services to influence public opinion. The community relations unit of the Army Information Division has begun to organize army advisory committees in each army area. Made up of community leaders in every walk of life—educators, churchmen, businessmen, veterans, editors, civic leaders, club women, labor leaders and farmers—these committees will eventually number 600 with 9,000 members scattered throughout the nation. As General Parks puts it:

> ... we disseminate Army policy to these committees through the Army commanders. Thus we make them members of our team. In turn they give us active support and advice such as in recruiting, in venereal disease control and in UMT. In addition, members of these committees are asked for reactions to various phases of the Army's program. This entails study and thought on their part; as they become indoctrinated themselves, they become our spokesmen. ...

ROTC courses afford opportunities to present the military viewpoint to the public; so do lectures and indoctrination courses given to reserve officers. These contacts also serve to convey to the military the reactions of civilians to their plans and programs. Liaison officers are maintained with committees of Congress (at their request); the legislative liaison divisions of the services are always ready to answer requests and to grant legitimate favors to Congressmen.

Specially detailed officers also maintain close relationships with the great veterans' organizations, the American Legion and the Veterans of Foreign Wars. They help the organizations to get speakers for their meetings and, in general, are active in presenting the military viewpoint. Semi-official associations endorsed by the Defense Departments—the Navy Industrial Association, the American Ordnance Association, the Air Force Association, the Navy League and others— maintain close links with industrialists and manufacturers, businessmen and others interested in military affairs.

Navy Day, Army Day and Air Force Day receive the full support of the services' nation-wide publicity organizations and are generally marked by parades or demonstrations in which the armed forces participate. Fraternal, social and religious clubs find the services helpful with speakers and literature when military subjects are scheduled for discussion. Cruises, indoctrination courses for civilians and businessmen, demonstrations and military pageantry of various kinds present the panorama of military life. And last, but not least in importance in a country which for the past half century has been made "advertising conscious," the services, through commercial agencies, are presenting—particularly in the interests of recruiting—an advertising appeal of nation-wide proportions. Such are the principal—but by no means all—ways by which the military present their point of view to the public.

They are effective ways. There can be no question that the American public today is better informed about, and more sympathetic to, military needs than ever before in peacetime. This does not mean, of course, that the services have become sacrosanct or immune to criticism. The public information media of the country are in no sense controlled by the military, nor do they hesitate to criticize—often viciously and sometimes ignorantly—the military viewpoint. Public opinion in other words has been, and is being, profoundly influenced by the military viewpoint, volubly and often ably, expressed, but it is not dominated by that viewpoint.

4. *Information or Propaganda?*

It is not easy to define with precision the role the military should have in the formulation of public opinion. With the dangers of the atomic age on one hand and our desire to preserve civil liberties on the other, we are between Scylla and Charybdis. On the one hand, it is essential—if the military is to remain strong in an age when military weakness may mean national death—that military facts and military opinion should be presented fully and effectively to government, legislators and public. On the other hand, if this presentation becomes twisted, too aggressive or too powerful, the military viewpoint may well dominate other viewpoints. In that case fundamental liberties would be lost, and our foreign policy might then become merely one of force, "force without stint, force without limit."

The middle road is always difficult to walk, particularly when dealing with public opinion. There is sometimes a very thin line between a frank presentation of the facts and cleverly manipulated propaganda. The Army, for instance, disavows propaganda as an instrument of public information and generally has followed the doctrine it preaches. General Parks has said: "We are concerned with creating and sustaining understanding and confidence—in short, public support. Our informative effort seeks to build the Armed Forces' prestige." The armed forces look upon their public relations and public information programs primarily as operations designed to further the goals of the military departments. Thus, the armed forces' public information activities may be, and often are, devoted to mobilizing opinion support for military policies already formulated, which usually, but not always, are in accord with other governmental policies. Such a concept of public relations obviously skirts dangerously close to propaganda.

Indeed, in the post-war years the services definitely have stepped across the line which divides proper publicity from propaganda. During the so-called "unification fight" all the services indulged in some open, and much covert, lobbying and in obvious propaganda designed to strengthen their cases. A Congressional sub-committee found the Army guilty of utilizing federal funds to influence Congress by producing motion pictures favoring universal military training and by hiring and sending around the country a civilian speaker who urged his audiences to influence their Congressmen to vote for the measure.[3] Such open-and-shut cases as these which transgress federal laws are easy to spot, and it can be said unequivocally that no such practices should be tolerated for a moment in a democracy which loves its freedom.

But there are other and borderline cases which are not so easily discerned. These involve the subtle use of the machinery of military information to present a partial or distorted view of our defense situation so as to form public opinion in a mould useful to military policy. An outstanding instance which has recurred again and again since the war is the loose use of statistics to prove our military weakness and Russia's great military strength. This propaganda is half-truth, and therefore cannot be refuted completely.

The technique is interesting. Statistics of Russian strength are assembled carefully and objectively by our intelligence services, but in the hands of public information officers or in the minds of top-ranking spokesmen for the services such data may become distorted and misleading. The Air Force, for instance, in attempts to secure public support for the reports of the President's Air Policy Commission and the Congressional Aviation Policy Board, let it be known to numerous newspapermen that Russia was operating some 14,000 combat planes and producing 40,000 to 50,000 planes annually. The best intelligence estimates indicate,

---

[3] See *New York Times*, July 24, 1947.

however, that only about 8,200 of Russia's 14,000 operating planes are combat types, and that the 40,000 to 50,000 figure for plane production referred to Russia's maximum *wartime* production; present production is put at about 6,000 to 12,000 annually. The Navy has issued somewhat similarly blown-up figures of Russian submarine strength and the Army has taken pains to maximize Russian ground strength and minimize our own (which, in truth, is small enough).

Now the services are fully justified—they are performing their duty—in calling public attention to their weaknesses and in requesting necessary remedial action. But they should present complete and accurate figures, not distorted ones, when making comparisons with foreign military strength. Furthermore, the proper forum for such a full presentation is Congress, not a dinner rostrum or a radio microphone. Irresponsible journalists, and newspapers which have an anti-Communist axe to grind, too often have aided and abetted the armed forces in presenting half-truths when comparing our strength with Russia's.

Misleading information gives the American public half-baked facts upon which it forms half-baked opinions. Even worse, it may force our foreign policy into a militaristic mould. In the past two years frequent statements, emphasizing our own military weakness and Russian military strength, have played directly into the hands of the Communists abroad. They have been quick to exploit the misleading information given out in Washington to strengthen their war of words and to increase Europe's fear that American aid would be "too little and too late."

The facts, all the facts, and impartial objective presentation of the facts should be, therefore, the first rule in the public information services of the Defense Departments.

There is a corollary to this rule. The public information organizations of the Defense Departments should be as small as possible; today they are unquestionably much too large. The New York offices, for instance, could easily be cut by one-third; the cut would not only increase efficiency and decrease expense but would automatically tend to limit operations to the essential task of giving out information. For no matter how good the intentions of the top echelons may be, these intentions are often subverted in practice by lower echelons. Hence, the information offices spend much of their time in essentially propagandistic roles—sponsoring Navy Day, for example. With reduced personnel they would, perforce, have to limit some of these extra-curricular activities, confining themselves to the information aspects of their job.

5. *New Forms of Civilian Control*

The proper function of the military in the formation of public opinion must be determined only on the highest levels. Are the chief public information officers of the services on a policy-making level? Do they have enough rank, prestige and position to make their voices heard in the formulation of policy, as well as in its execution? These officers—during and since the war—have been of high rank, respected in their profession, capable and sincere. Their abilities, personalities, character and background, of course, determine the degree to which they represent in their duties the narrow interest of their services or the broader interest of the nation and the people. Some of them have come to understand the meaning of a free press in a democracy. Some of them have learned to feel the public pulse and on many occasions they have represented the public interests, if not completely, yet with a far broader view than is usually found in General Staff deliberations. It is probably true that the top-ranking PIO officers have brought a tempering influence into the highest policy-making councils of their services. They have increased this influence by conducting periodically systematic surveys of national public opinion which they have disseminated widely through the service departments.

But public information chiefs, despite protestations to the contrary, are not completely on the policy-making levels. In many—indeed, in most instances—military policy, and particularly politico-military policy, is formed without asking the service experts how public opinion will receive the policy and how—from the public opinion point of view—it would be best executed. Our policy of aid to Greece, for instance, which got off to a bad start in Congress, would have been better received had the Army's Public Information Officer, after consultation with the State Department, secured from G-2 and released to the public available data about the foreign support given to Greek Communist guerrillas.

To give the chief public information officers of the services more influence in policy making, however, may endanger the essential control of the civilian over the military. Two of the three services maintain PIO organizations which are answerable directly to their civilian secretaries; the third—the Army's—is part of a special section of the General Staff and hence answerable to the Chief of Staff. Placing a service PIO directly under a civilian secretary has one disadvantage; in Washington a politically ambitious secretary may utilize the public information apparatus for his own advancement. Moreover, the arrangement does not insure complete civilian control; indeed, the most vigorous fighter for the civilian point of view that this writer has known in Washington, the officer who most consistently bucked the General Staff, was a PIO general who answered to the Chief of Staff. Nevertheless, the presentation of the military point of view to the public—and to other branches of government—is fundamentally the civilian secretary's job; the apparatus for his job should be directly under him, even though—at times —the secretary may be merely a mouthpiece for the General Staff.

But it is not sufficient to comply—within the National Military Establishment—with the forms of civilian control. Because, through these forms, a great amount of time, energy and information is devoted at public expense to bringing about a situation in which opinion in the country will be favorable to policies advocated by the military. Such a result may, or may not, be beneficial, depending upon whether or not the policies favored by the military are for the common good and whether or not they accord, or are in conflict, with the policies of the State Department or other branches of government.

It seems clear that the old forms of civilian control are not enough. Given the great importance of the military in the atomic age, and given the power of their information organizations over public opinion, it seems imperative that the activities of these organizations should be subject to continuous and minute scrutiny by Congress. A Congressional committee—perhaps a sub-committee of the Committee on Expenditures in the Executive Department—should concern itself exclusively with the public information agencies of government. This "watchdog of freedom" should exercise the same careful surveillance over the service PIO's that the Congressional Atomic Energy Committee exercises over the Atomic Energy Commission.

6. *The Question of Coordination*

There remains the cardinal problem of how best to coordinate the military publicity agencies with those of the State Department, the White House and other executive agencies. How can the public opinion experts in all government departments be brought together with top policy makers so that the effect of public opinion upon a proposed course of action can be considered along with other factors? How can a coordinated plan of explanation and interpretation be mapped out in which the military viewpoint has its rightful place? How, if it seems necessary, can a public opinion campaign be planned which will lay the facts motivating a government policy before the public, without resorting to propaganda?

The need for coordination of information activities does not have to be spelled out. Coordination was lacking in the Greek and Turkish aid programs, and in the Marshall Plan—hence the need to manufacture crises in order to move Congress to action. The ponderous mechanism of government often prevents the right hand from knowing what the left hand is doing; sometimes the military present facts to the public which undermine officially adopted policies. The Palestine mixup is a case in point. Partition was the policy officially adopted by this country in the Fall of 1947 after Presidential approval. Afterthoughts which stemmed in part from strategic considerations awoke doubts. In the Winter of 1947-48 military opinions, strenuously opposing partition and buttressed by facts, were presented to the public by military personnel or agencies. This intervention helped to change the policy, bringing about in the Spring of 1948 a virtual reversal of our prior stand. The reversal in turn was later reversed to the complete bewilderment of the world.

Regardless of the merits of the Palestine case, American foreign policy cannot be built on such shifting foundations; there must be consistency. This consistency can be achieved only by thorough meeting of minds in all agencies of government concerned with foreign affairs, before a new policy is enunciated. The best machinery for achieving this end appears to be the Cabinet and the new National Security Council. The National Security Council (see p. 101 above) is the proper agency for the coordination of military with foreign policy; it offers also the best top-level mechanism for coordination of all government public relations policies dealing with politico-military affairs. At such a level the broad outlines of national public information campaigns can be planned, and the right hand can be told what the left hand is doing.

The corollary to this is obvious; no policy should ever be recommended by the National Security Council until public opinion experts have been invited to give their estimates of how this policy will be accepted by the public, what effect it will have on national, and world, opinion. To insure that the citizen's point of view is represented in the National Security Council two key members of Congress, the chairmen of the Senate Committee on Foreign Relations and the House Committee on Foreign Affairs for instance, might be invited to sit on special occasions as advisory members of the Security Council, at least in all discussions of public opinion. In the Security Council the primacy of civilian, as opposed to military, control is assured by vesting final decision, in case of uncompromising disagreement, in the President himself.

7. *Picture of the Military Mind*

A governmental information program such as has been suggested would be open to dangerous abuse if it fell into the hands of unscrupulous men, or if it were manipulated to the advantage of a particular group in government, and not in the national interest. In that case information could become propaganda for, as we have seen, only a thin line divides them.

It is of fundamental importance that the military mind should influence but should never dominate public opinion programs. With some persuasiveness, it has been claimed that there is no such thing as "the military mind," and it is true that the term has been generalized and misapplied. But there is a scientific mind; there is a religious mind; there is a creative mind; there is even (and quite definitely) a stockbroker's mind! And there is a military mind.

The military mind is the product of its training and thought processes and environment—and sometimes of its heritage. It has assets and it has liabilities. It is a rational mind but not an intuitive one. It is a pragmatic mind. It is a mind disciplined to obedience and to order, to system and to logic. But it is also a mind accustomed to the habit of command, taught to think fundamentally in terms of physical power. It can grapple with tangibles but not so well with intangibles.

The military mind finds expression in some officers—a minority, particularly those who never rise above colonel's rank—in a "yes-man" attitude. It is expressed in others—a minority of those whose collars show one or two stars—in an almost arrogant sureness toward subordinates. These officers do not hesitate to overrule experts or to maintain opinions unsupported by knowledge and experience. The military mind can be—and often is—an insulated mind. Modern educational methods in the services, and the impact of total war upon military thinking, which has required a broader grasp of non-military subjects than ever before in history, have destroyed some of this insularity. But far too many officers are still immured behind the Maginot Line of their mental narrowness.

The military mind—a mind spent in the lifetime study of war—is obviously not well adapted to dealing with the arts of peace. The habit of command and the compulsions of discipline are attributes that seem out of place in the disorderly give-and-take, the hugger-mugger and free-swinging of political Washington. To the military mind the civilian is too often a creature apart. Civilian opinion, undisciplined, unstable and swayed by emotion, is a phenomenon to be "controlled."

The military mind, in brief, often is not fundamentally a democratic mind. No military organization can be democratic and still retain its essential military characteristics; the two are antithetical.

The influence of the military on public opinion—a necessary influence in the atomic age—has reached the point today where it is time to call a halt. The military viewpoint does not dominate public opinion, but, essential though it is, it has reached a point where much further extension of it could be dangerous at home and abroad. In the formulation of foreign policy, the military mind and military opinion are essential ingredients, but if the military mind dominates, over any long-term period, war is very likely to result. There must always be, in the military concept of our foreign relations, a potential enemy. Before the war our military men were careful to label this enemy "Yellow" or "Green" or "Blue"; since the war Russia has been the open and avowed opponent—a gain for realism, but at a cost in tension.

The military mind is little suited to deal with so vast and important an intangible as public opinion. Military opinion must be presented to the public; military facts must influence foreign policy but civilian and non-military control must always be maintained. Otherwise we may lose those things which we strive to defend.

CHAPTER SIX

MORE THAN DIPLOMACY

By W. Phillips Davison

THE PRESIDENT, the Congress and the military are important influences in making foreign policy and in moulding public opinion about that policy. But the basic agency is, of course, the State Department. That is why, as has been said, the Department has the ranking place in this book. That is why its opinion operations should be studied in greater detail than any of the others. This chapter is such a study of the State Department's operations in the field of opinion at home.

The functions of the Department with regard to public opinion in the nation are largely organized in the Office of Public Affairs, under jurisdiction of the Assistant Secretary of State for Public Affairs. In this office are several divisions dealing with special fields.[1] The functions at home are twofold:

First there are the *intelligence functions*. The Department must know what people are thinking about foreign policy. It has to gauge public opinion to determine what policies do have widespread support and what policies do not. It has to discover and classify the areas of ignorance

[1] See Chart A on next page, describing the set-up as of January 20, 1949, when Secretary Acheson took over. It was expected that he would make a number of structural changes to consolidate the various phases of the information operation. Such a reorganization constitutes a long step in the right direction; yet what is needed, as this book attempts to demonstrate, is more than structural reorganization. What is also needed is a change in spirit that will give the public opinion operations its proper place in the work of the Department.

CHART A

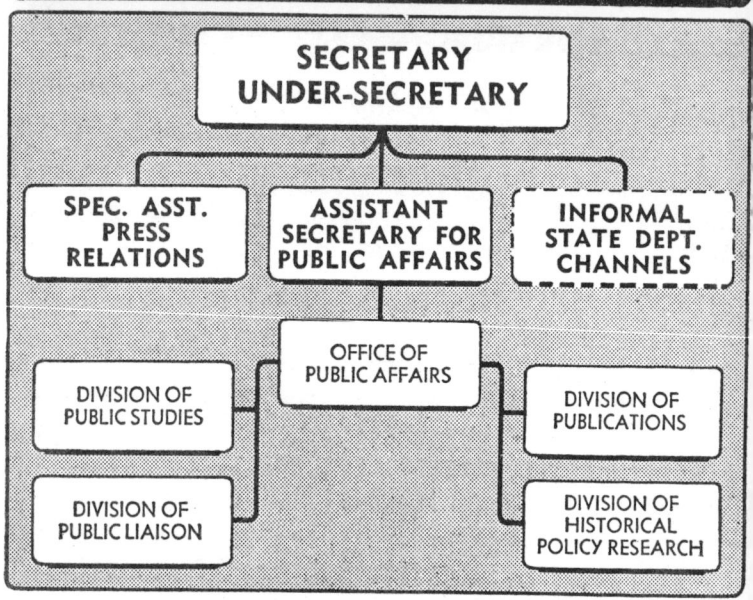

THE STATE DEPARTMENT SET-UP FOR THE OPINION OPERATION AT HOME

(This is the set-up as of January 20, 1949. Some structural changes were then expected with the advent of Secretary Acheson.)

THE SECRETARY AND UNDER-SECRETARY of State set the broad lines of policy of our intelligence and information programs at home.

SPECIAL ASSISTANT FOR PRESS RELATIONS channels day-to-day news to the correspondents, releases texts of statements or speeches by State Department officials, arranges interviews for correspondents with the Secretary and other high officials.

INFORMAL STATE DEPARTMENT CHANNELS include the Counselor, the Policy Planning staff, the Assistant Secretaries and others who give off-the-record interviews to the press.

OFFICE OF PUBLIC AFFAIRS operates in a variety of fields to disseminate information and to measure opinion. It works through four divisions:

Division of Public Studies surveys newspapers, magazines, radio transcripts, public opinion polls, etc. in an attempt to learn what the American people are thinking about foreign affairs.

(Continued on bottom of next page.)

about policies already in effect and policies about to be formulated. This does not mean that the Department should slavishly follow the popular fads of the day; it does mean that policy officials must be apprised of existing opinion trends if they are to provide sound leadership in the field of foreign policy.

Second there are the *information functions*. The Department must have the personnel, the organization, the technical skill and the authority to inform public opinion, to replace ignorance with knowledge, suspicion with confidence. It has to do this if the average man is to recognize his interest in, and identify himself with, the country's policy.

1. *The Intelligence Functions*

The Office of Public Affairs uses four main methods to investigate and analyze what people are thinking. They are: (a) a systematic study of current publications and public opinion polls; (b) analysis of letters written to the Department; (c) liaison with citizens' organizations and other groups interested in public affairs; (d) the informal channels—the contacts of State Department officials with the public.

a. *Publications and Polls*

Watching publications and public opinion polls is the business of the Division of Public Studies, set up as a unit of the Office of Public Affairs in 1944. In the attempt to learn what people are thinking about foreign affairs and policy,

---

(*Continued from bottom of preceding page.*)

Division of Public Liaison maintains contact with various groups such as veterans, farmers and businessmen, explains policy to these groups and reports on their reactions.

Division of Publications prints and distributes pamphlets and booklets, diplomatic documents, speeches by Department members and official studies and reports.

Division of Historical Policy Research prepares studies and compilations in the field of American foreign policy, maintains the Department's library.

the Division uses the following principal sources of information:

Editorials, columns and feature articles from some 225 daily newspapers representing all shades in the political spectrum.

The *Congressional Record.*

Findings of the three best known public opinion agencies—the American Institute of Public Opinion, the *Fortune* poll, and the National Opinion Research Center. State and local polls are studied, as well as polls on specific questions of foreign policy.

Approximately 60 magazines and periodicals.

Transcripts of radio comment.

Statements issued by political, business, labor leaders, etc., particularly statements by members of Congress on questions of foreign policy.

Resolutions and publications of private organizations—economic, religious, educational, veterans', etc.

The intelligence derived from these sources is to some extent correlated with that obtained through the other channels.

b. *The Mail Bag*

Mail directed to the Department of State as well as White House mail dealing with foreign affairs is handled by the Public Inquiries Branch of the Office of Public Affairs. The flow is extremely irregular. On an average Public Inquiries receives 400 letters per day, but when major foreign policies are under public discussion the number may increase sharply. In 1944 and 1945 two-thirds of all mail dealing with foreign affairs was addressed to the White House. Since that time the situation has been reversed. In 1947 and 1948, two-thirds of such mail has been addressed to the State Department.[2]

---

[2] About 80 percent of original letters, excluding form letters, went directly to the State Department.

The subjects dealt with in correspondence are those currently featured in headlines and on the radio. In the week of November 22 to 26, 1948, 970 communications were received, including 101 form letters and 869 personal letters. The subjects with which these dealt were:

Palestine	Displaced persons
China	Soviet Union
United Nations	Germany
Spain	Department of State

In addition to the flood of letters received and answered by the Public Inquiries Branch, operating and policy-making offices carry on an extensive correspondence with Congressmen and private citizens in which Department policies are explained and justified.

Liaison with Citizens' Groups

The Department pays special attention to requests or communications from citizens' organizations and groups. When a large organization sends in a query or resolution dealing with foreign policy, the document is often duplicated and circulated to policy officials throughout the Department. Expressions of opinion from important religious, veterans', labor, farm and business groups are not dismissed lightly.

In many cases, the Division of Public Liaison sends a representative to the national conventions of these groups, and this representative is required to make a report on the opinions expressed there which have a bearing upon the State Department's sphere of activities. Similarly, the Division arranges background conferences in New York and Washington for the press or legislative representatives of these groups, and on such occasions the flow of information is two-way. The Department attempts to explain its policy, but at the same time pays close attention to the types of questions asked and the attitudes revealed by the group representatives.

d. *Personal Contact with the Public*

The Department as a whole also attempts to learn what the public is thinking by personal contacts of its officers, from various branches and divisions, who go out from Washington to attend conferences, to make speeches and to talk with representative citizens. These trips are particularly useful in reorienting foreign service officers who have been long stationed abroad.

Prominent citizens serving as advisers to the Department help keep it informed on public attitudes. Newspapermen in interviewing members of the Department, through their questions and in private conversation, often convey strong impressions of what the public is thinking. The news stories they write also give insights into the attitudes of those on the outside.

High officials of the Department usually are on fairly close terms with certain Congressmen, and even a passing word from a legislator as to what the public wants—particularly if he is a member of a foreign relations or an appropriations committee—makes a deep impression.

2. *Reports for Policy Makers*

These are the most important of the Department's intelligence sources at home. They form the foundation of the whole intelligence operation. Based on the material received, the Public Studies Division issues periodic reports to policy-forming officers in the Department and to our embassies abroad. These reports include:

> *A daily summary of opinion,* a two- or three-page document, sent to over fifty officials in the Department.
>
> *A fortnightly summary,* in ten or fifteen pages, of American opinion on international affairs. Approximately 200 copies are distributed within the Department, and twice that number are sent to our embassies abroad.

A weekly digest of outstanding magazine articles relating to international affairs. This digest, devoting approximately half a page to each article, reaches some 80 members of the Department.

A weekly summary of the opinions and attitudes of American private organizations and groups interested in foreign affairs, such as the A.F. of L., the C.I.O., the National Association of Manufacturers, the U. S. Chamber of Commerce. About 50 copies are circulated in the Department.

The Division also issues special reports when required, summarizing public opinion on particular subjects such as aid to Europe, our occupation policy in Germany and Japan, policy toward Russia, the program for the control of atomic energy. It often sends telegrams to American delegates at international conferences to let them know what the American public thinks about the issues they are discussing.

The following extract from a daily report illustrates how the Division summarizes press opinion:

Mme. Chiang arrived in Washington "for what looked like a forlorn attempt to get more American help for her husband's government," the *Wash. Post* reports—an observation shared by many. The *N. Y. Her. Trib.* cautions that the answer to her appeals "will have to be founded on facts, many of them harsh and unpleasant, and probably cannot be in all respects the answer which she would like to hear." Her visit prompts renewed statements of opposition to large-scale aid from the *Nation, New Republic, N. Y. Star* and *Sioux Falls Argus-Leader.* "It may well be that in the interest of world freedom the U. S. should comply with Mme. Chiang's request," says the *Phila. Inquirer,* "but we should make no such agreement without receiving absolute assurance that the Nationalist Govt. will institute basic reforms which will make it truly democratic and truly popular." However, the *Des Moines Reg.* urges the U. S. not to "kid" itself that aid to Chiang can help make China democratic, asserting: "The reason for aid to Chiang—and it may well be compelling—is purely and simply to support a potential military ally."

The Office of Public Affairs interprets its findings cautiously; it rarely makes recommendations with regard to policy. Instead it tries to present in capsule form a summary of public attitudes for consideration as one element in framing policy. The Office also attempts to define the areas in which the public is badly informed, and as a result has no opinion.

3. *Appraisal of the Intelligence Service*

There is a constant stream of information coming into the Office of Public Affairs and there is also a constant stream of reports and summaries going out to the policy-making officials of the Department. Two big questions now arise: How complete and accurate is the intelligence obtained? and How much of the material is used by the policy makers?

With regard to Question No. 1 it should first be pointed out that present methods of opinion testing are not sufficiently sensitive to enable anyone to predict exactly the trend of opinion. The staff available is too small, moreover, to take full advantage of the best techniques of studying public opinion. Hence, public reactions on many issues remain unexplored; others can be appraised only superficially. Because of these deficiencies, the surveys of the Office of Public Affairs are often inconclusive. For example, it may find that 80 percent of the population has heard of a given issue, and of this 60 percent approves American policy; that the majority of newspaper columnists and editorial writers, on the other hand, oppose it; and that large national organizations have refrained from expressing opinions. Further, it may find that those who are best informed tend to be opposed, while those who are less well informed tend to favor the policy.

Thus further analysis of the findings would make them more useful. Although there is some correlation of the reports, as a general rule intelligence regarding public opinion is passed on to the policy maker as a digest of what people are saying, rather than an analysis of why they think as they do. Policy makers are therefore frequently left to draw conflicting or contradictory conclusions from the same opinion reports.

With regard to Question No. 2—how much is the intelligence used?—there is conflict between theory and practice. Former Secretary Marshall stated the theory in this way:

> The Department of State welcomes public scrutiny of its efforts and the criticism which helps us to check the wisdom of our actions. We try in every possible way to find out what the American public thinks about the great issues before us and to explain to them what we think and do about them. . . . Letters from organizations and individuals, which we received in great numbers, we carefully studied. No organization or individual expressing opinions or judgments on important public issues should conclude that such views are of no interest or assistance. The contrary is the case.[3]

But are officials who study public opinion actually consulted when it comes to deciding matters of high policy? Is their information taken into consideration? In short, what role does American public opinion now play in formulating foreign policy?

Public opinion aspects of policy receive in practice far less attention than political, economic and legal considerations. The Geographic Offices,[4] which are the pivotal points in the formulation of foreign policy, usually are the first to receive major communications from our diplomats abroad. Before making recommendations for action these offices, or their subdivisions, are responsible for consulting other appropriate offices and divisions and for considering all relevant factors. Now, since the Geographic Offices as a rule include no public opinion specialists, we might assume that they would seek advice from officials who are in touch with public atti-

---

[3] Remarks before the American Association for the United Nations, September 14, 1947.
[4] See Chapter One, p. 28. While the observations made here result from study of the role of domestic opinion in foreign policy, the majority of them apply as strongly, and in some cases more strongly, to the role of foreign opinion, which is discussed in Chapter Eight.

tudes. But this happens only to a limited extent. It is true that most of the officials in the Geographic Offices read the reports on domestic public opinion. Sometimes they send documents to the public opinion experts for comment, and sometimes these experts serve on Departmental committees alongside representatives of the Geographic Offices, or maintain informal contact with them. Nevertheless, in actual operations these offices ordinarily give only slight attention to the public opinion aspect. Their contacts with the offices concerned with public attitudes have remained rudimentary. A recent analysis of working documents passing through the State Department indicated that 95 percent of all policy documents were not even shown to the public opinion officers. No wonder these officers complain that they usually learn of even the most important policies only after their formulation is complete, ready for public release in a matter of hours.

In the higher reaches of the Department, formal machinery for coordination exists, but this machinery is not used effectively. High-level committees, it is true, often include the directors of the public opinion offices, and the Assistant Secretary for Public Affairs meets with all other assistant secretaries and officers of equivalent rank. But in such meetings public opinion officials are at a disadvantage since their subordinates usually have not been permitted to collaborate in preparing policy papers, whereas their opposite numbers have been kept informed during every stage of planning. Also, important policies sometimes by-pass the higher committees on their way to the Secretary's office or come up for only cursory discussion after decisions have already been made informally.

In practice a policy maker may be more influenced by reading his customary newspaper in the evening and thinking through the arguments advanced by columnists or commentators than by scanning in his office mimeographed reports on public opinion.

Many high officials in the Department, even those who recognize the importance of taking public attitudes into account, discount the need for expert advice. One of them has said: "We don't need to call in the experts on information; we know pretty well what the public is thinking." Franklin D. Roosevelt and former Secretary of State James F. Byrnes were often able with remarkable accuracy to predict the public reaction to a proposed policy. But most officials who affect this sixth sense use it largely as an excuse for disregarding other testimony, especially when projects in which they are interested appear to be at variance with formal analyses of public opinion.

Finally there are the traditions, the habits and the customs of State Department practice which prejudice many officials in the policy-making branches against paying great heed to the advice of the division concerned with public opinion.

Nevertheless, taking into account appalling deficiencies in manpower and skilled technicians, it should be recognized that a start has been made toward collecting the information on domestic knowledge and attitudes necessary for conducting a sound democratic foreign policy.[5] But it is only a start. To be fully effective the intelligence section of the Office of Public Affairs must have a staff of experts who will not only collect intelligence on American public opinion but who will evaluate and assess it for the policy makers.

Finally, there must be a general reorientation of State Department thinking with regard to public opinion so that policy makers will play hunches less frequently and make use of experts' advice more consistently.

[5] There is, at least, an infinite improvement over five years ago. Joseph M. Jones, a former State Department official, in his book, *A Modern Foreign Policy for the United States* (*op. cit.*, p. 52), wrote:

"The State Department's facilities for finding out what the American people are thinking and hoping on matters of foreign policy (or on any other matter) are nonexistent. There is no analysis of current information carried on in the Department. The press is not systematically read and analyzed for trends; current literature is not studied. In addition to this, Department officers are among the most insulated of all government personnel from the influence of American life and thinking. . . ."

4. *The Information Functions*

The State Department relies on three principal channels to inform the public at home.

(a) The most important channel is the press (including radio and magazines, as well as newspapers).

(b) A secondary channel is provided by the Department's own publications, which are handled by the Publications Division.

(c) A third channel is the Public Liaison Division which sends out speakers to address citizens' organizations and other groups in all parts of the country.

a. *The Press*

There have been four State Department sources, three formal and one informal, available to newspapermen, radio reporters and magazine writers.

The Press Relations Office. This has been directed by a Special Assistant responsible to the Secretary of State. The office has conducted primarily a service operation—the distribution of mimeographed news releases (about 1,000 separate items a year) and texts of statements or speeches by high officials; the arranging of press conferences with the Secretary and other policy-making officers; and, in general, the performance of day-to-day news functions.

The Press Conference. Ever since William Jennings Bryan's tenure, the press conference with the Secretary has been a Department fixture. Until recent years a press conference was held each day; Charles Evans Hughes[6] held two a day. When the Department was headed by Secretaries Byrnes and Marshall, the conference was a weekly affair, held each Wednesday at noon in the auditorium of the State Department building. Generally about seventy-five correspondents

---

[6] When he was Secretary, Mr. Hughes regarded the press conference as the most important function of his day as Secretary. He later told a correspondent that the Secretary of State performed a real service to the country when he approached the press conference "in a responsible frame of mind."

attended. The conference started promptly, usually with the reading of a prepared statement by the Secretary (or the Under-Secretary if the Secretary was unable to attend). Then there was a question period. Quite frequently questions brought answers such as "I can't say" or "No comment on that one." But sometimes a good question would bring out important background material.

The Office of Public Affairs. This has been primarily a source for material for magazine writers and scholars who are not interested in day-to-day news.

Private Interviews. Aside from these formal channels, correspondents, to an increasing extent, have found that both news and more complete and authoritative background information can be obtained by talking privately with various high officials. The result is that many front-page news stories regarding State Department affairs are based on the remarks of the Counselor or some other high official.

b. *Publications*

The State Department's Publications Division prints and distributes many pamphlets and booklets to inform the public. These include important diplomatic documents, speeches made by members of the Department and official studies and reports. Some of these are difficult reading; for example, such formidable documents as *The International Control of Atomic Energy: Scientific Information Transmitted to the United Nations Atomic Energy Commission,* or *The Paris Conference of the Council of Foreign Ministers.* These documents are not ordinarily issued in large numbers—usually 1,000 to 10,000 copies—but they provide much solid information. Writers and radio commentators use them for background articles. They are also useful to college professors, student and special study groups.

The State Department *Bulletin,* a weekly magazine edited in the Office of Public Affairs, covers most of the non-confidential activities of the State Department. Its 3,500 subscribers include several hundred engaged in journalism, radio, or some other activity which involves passing along information about foreign policy and interpreting it to the public. The *Bulletin* contains statements by officials, reports of Departmental activities and articles on international affairs on a wide variety of topics such as *The World Talks Over Its Food and Agriculture Program* and *American Interest in International Motor Travel*.

c. *Citizens' Organizations and Departmental Speakers*

Americans who take a more than average interest in foreign policy usually are members of one or more national organizations, either of a research or propaganda nature, which put out information on international issues, conduct discussions, and pass resolutions—organizations such as the National Foreign Trade Council, the National Association of Manufacturers and the League of Women Voters. The State Department, recognizing that an appreciable proportion of the population absorbs its information and opinions on foreign policy from such organizations, has established facilities to service them.

The Public Liaison Division maintains contact with more than 300 national citizens' groups, with a combined membership running into many millions. The Division assists them in getting speakers, supplies information, helps their delegates obtain passports for travel abroad, sends representatives to their conventions and provides discussion materials. Several State Department publications, issued with the needs of large organizations in mind, are distributed in quantity to groups which request them. These include *Foreign Affairs Outlines*—brief, popularly written summaries, with titles such as "What Are We Doing in Germany and Why"—and *Pocket Pamphlets* which give concise summaries of the United States position on such issues as atomic energy and international trade. During the fiscal year 1947, the Department put out almost three million items of this kind.

To keep national organizations abreast of foreign policy, conferences at which officials discuss current issues informally with 40 or 50 delegates are planned. Occasionally, more formal meetings are arranged, with several hundred present. In such conferences the Public Liaison Division aims to achieve two-way communication with the national organizations, to provide information to them and to receive suggestions and reactions from them.

During the fiscal year 1947, the Department received 1,940 requests for speakers and supplied 878. Their immediate audiences totaled close to half a million. Several million more heard them over the radio. About 15,000 letters a year are sent by the Department to private citizens who have requested information on foreign policy. With most of these replies, relevant Departmental publications concerning the question at issue are enclosed.

5. *Appraisal of the Information Service*

The Department does try, as we have seen, to keep the public informed through the three principal channels—the press, its own publications and liaison with citizens' organizations. But there are many criticisms of its information functions. Some of these criticisms are directed to the Department itself; others arise from circumstances over which the Department has no control. These criticisms fall into three general categories: (a) Weak coordination; (b) poor relations between the press and high officials; (c) poor planning in the release of information.

a. *Weak coordination.* To avoid conflicts in statements emanating from various sources it would seem desirable that a single official, or office, should be responsible for seeing that correspondents and the public can obtain a complete, realistic view of every important new development. No adequate provision of this sort has been made to date. On the contrary, each unit of the Department has been largely responsible for initiating its own news releases, and there has been no common information policy to guide all of them. Concentration of responsibility for giving out information would help, also, to bring a better balance in publicity, preventing one section of the Department from flooding the public with information, while another equally important section remains silent because of inertia, the traditional tendency of a bureaucracy to keep out of trouble by saying as little as possible. Under present conditions the silent offices have many excuses: some are pressed for time; others consider public relations less important than their other activities; still others, since implementation of major policies is divided among many divisions and offices, may be uncertain as to who should originate the release.

b. *Poor relations between press and high officials.* A clearer understanding is needed of the responsibility of high officials of the Department in their relations with representatives of the press. The Counselor and certain other leading officials, as we have observed, serve informally as extremely important sources of information. Correspondents who have come to rely on talking frequently with these officials feel that the Department is holding back information when occasionally they are denied interviews. Yet, from the point of view of the officials concerned, such action may be fully justified.

Most Department officials are overburdened with other duties; the function of giving out information has not been formally delegated to them, and when they talk with newsmen it is usually on their own time. One such official recently remarked to the writer: "I've been meeting with reporters from time to time as a personal favor; it's not part of my job. But when I'm tired at the end of the day and want to go home and rest, they act insulted because I won't talk to them."

This situation would seem to indicate the need of improving regular channels of information, so as to reduce pressure on overworked higher officials. But this does not mean that high officials should not see reporters; on the contrary, a part of their time should be allocated to meeting with representatives of the press.

The reluctance of career members of the State Department to discuss official business with the press or to be involved in publicity of any kind can easily be understood. Among the facts with which they are dealing there is always some dynamite, and it is just this explosive material which the reporter wants. Hence, the official has been trained in caution. If he speaks inadvisedly, his career may be ruined.

Foreign correspondents who have covered the Foreign Office in London report that the British civil servant appears to be able to combine a high degree of discretion with a high degree of communicativeness. The sharp contrast with American methods was seen at the San Francisco Conference. American officials often had to check with higher authority before answering queries, while their British counterparts were able to answer the same questions immediately.

c. *Poor planning of the release of information.* Not infrequently a new line of policy does not accord with information previously released, or it may be expressed in such a way as to assume too much knowledge on the part of the public. Background information enabling the public to understand the reasons for the new policy is not usually released in advance. On the contrary the new policy is often exploded over the heads of a public too startled to understand it. Several months later the background information will appear in State Department publications.

Under these conditions each major policy "release," e.g., the Greek-Turkish Aid Program or the Marshall Plan, creates a minor crisis within the information offices; they are flooded with questions which they are not prepared to answer.

Plans for informing the public should be an integral part of policy making. Whenever possible, background information should be released before the policy is announced. The

New York Times observed editorially (September 15, 1947) with regard to the Greek-Turkish Aid Program:

> There was not, for example, an adequate preparation of public opinion for the steps taken under the Truman Doctrine of last March. The steps were logical and defensible. Yet they surprised most members of Congress and it was more than two weeks before their relationship to United Nations principles and policies was officially explained.

Release of preparatory or background information, because of possible effects upon diplomatic negotiations, must be the result of joint thinking of all those concerned with the policy.

Ways of presenting a policy in popular form should be worked out. Many policies have been released to the public in highly technical language which is unclear to the layman. Former Secretary Hull sometimes expressed irritation with press correspondents because, failing to "read between the lines," they did not grasp the full implications of diplomatic lingo. Yet the information officer, or the newspaperman, hesitates to rephrase an official statement of policy for fear of altering its meaning.

The policy-making group, anticipating questions, should decide in advance what can and what cannot be told. Traditionally, the State Department has told as little as possible. Recently the attitude has begun to change, but official answers still show little evidence that questions have had extensive prior consideration. If a press relations officer is put on the spot, he often refers his interrogator to a policy official. The latter also is in a difficult position. The formulation of the policy in question may have required the consideration of a dozen or more experts. Any one of them, confronted by a newspaperman, naturally hesitates to commit the others. So he either has to dismiss his questioner with "no comment," or else give his personal opinion "off the record." This dilemma could often be avoided if questions were anticipated and discussed during the process of policy formulation.

The handling of the publicity on the Marshall Plan illustrates some of these defects in planning. It is true that in a speech in Cleveland, Mississippi, May 8, 1947, Dean Acheson, then Under Secretary, had called attention to Europe's need for further economic assistance. Also a few widely read journalists, like James Reston and Walter Lippmann, had foreseen the new policy. But after the Plan had been publicly announced in former Secretary Marshall's Harvard speech on June 5, 1947, the publicity bogged down. Violent arguments arose within the Department as to how much and what kind of information should be released, and different offices and officials released conflicting and incomplete bits of news. The Press Relations Office distributed mimeographed texts of the Harvard speech and of several related speeches, but was unsure how much more information could be disclosed. Policy officials gave additional data to members of the press, but without informing the Press Relations Office. The Office of Public Affairs arranged for several officials to make clear statements in a radio broadcast, but these statements failed to find their way into the newspapers. Other officials who suggested making clarifying statements were overruled by their superiors. Newspaper correspondents and experts on foreign affairs were confused and exasperated. The result was that for several months the American people failed to get a broadly based appreciation of this great new departure in American policy.

6. One Basic Recommendation

Out of this examination of the operations of the intelligence and information functions of the State Department, as they relate to American public opinion, one basic recommendation seems to emerge: What is needed is one responsible head—a man of ability, experience and decision—who could run the whole operation with the complete confidence of the Secretary. That man presumably would be the Assistant Secretary for Public Affairs.

The Assistant Secretary and his key divisional heads should participate in policy discussions. They should be taken into confidence as soon as a new policy comes under consideration, and the program of public information should be studied along with the program of foreign policy. Information policy cannot be worked out after the fact; it must be planned in advance.

Finally the Assistant Secretary needs a large and expert staff—much larger than he has now—if the job is to be done properly. He ought to have topnotch specialists—skilled publicists and public opinion analysts. Obviously these cannot be had for small salaries, and they cannot be retained if they are to be subject to unfounded character besmirching.

In the last analysis the success or failure of the Department's information program will depend on the caliber of the men who are available to conduct it. Every effort should be made to attract and retain such men.

PART TWO

FOREIGN POLICY AND OPINION ABROAD

These chapters evaluate the public opinion problem abroad; they indicate its proportions through a survey of European opinion about us and an analysis of Communist propaganda activities; they describe the opinion operation as it is carried on, first by the government, and second by private enterprise; they appraise the effectiveness of the operation; and they make some suggestions for its improvement.

CHAPTER SEVEN

CHART OF THE COLD WAR [1]

By Shepard Stone

THE JOB of enlightenment confronting the United States abroad is complex and elusive. It is far easier to supply the physical wants of hundreds of millions of men and women, still carrying burdens left by the war, than to win them over psychologically.

American production, American dollars, wheat, automobiles and machinery undoubtedly constitute a mighty force in helping to create good will toward us. Nevertheless, despite American aid flowing to many countries, there is considerable suspicion abroad of our motives and perplexity about our policies. In every European country there is a latent anti-American feeling compounded of envy and fear, and the Communists make the most of this situation.

In Asia, too, the job before us is becoming increasingly complex. Here are hundreds of millions of people, living largely in poverty, who seek a minimum of economic security and also independence of the white colonial powers. Here is rich ground for Communism.

All over the world, it becomes more and more apparent, the same basic conflict is developing. For the present, still, the primary area is Europe, and it is there that the heaviest efforts in the propaganda battle have been made. For that

---

[1] This chapter as well as chapters eight, nine and ten are based in part on reports from thirty-four American correspondents in Europe of the *New York Times*, the *New York Herald Tribune*, the National Broadcasting Company, the Columbia Broadcasting System and *Time*, Inc. Their names and organizations are listed on p. x.

reason emphasis is placed in this and in the following chapters on the struggle for the mind of Europe.

In analyzing our job in Europe—the critical area in the struggle against Russia—we must take into account these four considerations:

1.) How is European opinion formed?
2.) What is European opinion of us and of Russia?
3.) What is the Communist method in influencing it?
4.) What, consequently, are the challenges we face?

1. *How European Opinion Is Formed*

The history book, as well as more recent events and today's headlines, plays a tremendous role in the formation of European thinking and attitudes.

History is a living thing in Europe. We cannot understand the impact of current events on the European mind without exploring fundamental attitudes—political, social and religious—which have grown out of a thousand years of European history and European traditions. Some of these basic attitudes have no counterpart in the United States, for our development as a people and a nation has been relatively free of the fears and hatreds which burden Europe. For example, the deeply implanted French fear of Germany—born out of bitter memories of invasions from across the Rhine—colors France's entire attitude toward European reconstruction. Hence any American move to revive post-war Germany breeds hostility toward the United States. Similarly, the hatred of the Russians and the Poles for the Germans, and *vice versa,* goes far back to the days when Teuton and Slav fought for the Eastern outposts of Europe. Aid to Greece stirs bitterness among the ancient Balkan enemies of that country. These historical pressures, and hundreds of others, must be taken into account in any policy relating to Europe.

It is against this background of tradition and prejudice that we must assess the importance of the agencies and media which lead and form public opinion in Europe. In Europe, even more than in this country, the church, trade unions, fraternal organizations and political parties (anchored far more strongly to ideologies than ours) exert a strong influence on their members.

Nevertheless, in Europe, east as well as west of the Iron Curtain, the newspaper and radio, just as in this country, are the most important influences in spreading information. The newspaper has first importance for, measured against American standards, relatively few Europeans own radios. This is true even though newspapers in Europe, with a few outstanding exceptions, are not so highly developed as organs of information and news as in this country.

In Europe, in the countries where they are permitted to circulate, American newspapers and magazines with their more complete reports are read by a small but influential group. Our publications, with the exception of official matter, are not allowed to circulate in Soviet Russia nor in Russian-dominated countries.

Although radio plays a lesser role than newspapers in Europe its impact is important. There is evidence from many surveys that although the number of radio sets is small there are many listeners for each set. The information they impart gains wide currency through word-of-mouth or grapevine channels.

In the countries behind the Iron Curtain, foreign broadcasts play a large role despite the limited audience, for they frequently provide the only news that is not sifted by Communist propaganda agencies.

Finally, there is the motion picture. Since European movie production lags behind American, the American film is seen as frequently in Europe as the indigenous. And many American films give Europeans an unreal view of this country.

Such are the historical and present-day influences that mould public opinion in Europe. What is that opinion today, particularly as it concerns the United States and Russia?

2. *European Opinion of Us—and of Russia*

Obviously we do not know and cannot determine precisely what goes on in the minds and hearts of 400,000,000 Europeans. Nevertheless, the following general conclusions may be drawn:

(a) Public opinion in Europe is determined primarily by the struggle for food and shelter. The fundamental urge is to recover from the wreckage of war, to rise up out of the ruins.

(b) Europeans prefer personal freedom to dictatorial restrictions. They prefer freedom of speech to suppression. But, wherever there must be a choice between economic security and personal freedom, there are extremely strong pressures to give precedence to economic security.

(c) Europeans, in general, desire American aid, but at the same time they do not want a showdown with Soviet Russia, unless the United States is militarily prepared to stand up against Moscow. That is why many peoples in Western Europe want a hard-and-fast military guarantee from this country and will remain skeptical of our friendship until they receive one. Economic help from the United States is a tremendous psychological factor, but it does not dispel the fear of the Russian army on the frontiers of Western and Central Europe.

(d) Although the majority of Europeans west of Russia are anti-Communist, many no longer believe that a rigid capitalist system can restore political security or cure their economic or social ills. In their own countries they have adopted, in greater or less degree, the mechanisms of Socialism. Ideologically, however, this vast group of people adheres to the American conception of liberties and human rights.

There is in Europe a not inconsiderable area of understanding of the United States among the more intelligent, better informed groups, but there are also wide areas of ignorance and deep pools of prejudice. For example, here is a description of French attitudes—which are fairly typical of general European attitudes—toward the United States:

First, foremost and almost unanimous, in every class of French society, is the opinion that America is a sprawling giant only recently conscious of its enormous power and lacking the emotional balance and experience to harness this great force and direct it for progress, peace and prosperity. Along with this is the impression, widely held, that America is almost totally lacking in culture.

There is considerable envy in France of America's abundance of food and mechanical contrivances. In pre-war days there was a certain scorn for our push-button civilization. Dirt and hunger and the difficulties of post-war life, however, have begun to change France's former disdain for modern conveniences.

The pre-war idea of the loud-mouthed, naive, somewhat vulgar and bad-mannered Babbitt on vacation is still prevalent in many circles. Post-war tourists are not helping to correct that idea in any important degree.

There is, however, a positive side to the picture. France has been greatly impressed by American literature. Also, there is the French admiration for American efficiency, not the soulless efficiency of the Germans, which the French detest, but the rather friendly, easy-going, yet productive methods of the Americans, from top corporation men down through foremen and workers.[2]

And a correspondent in London reports:

Britain wants nothing more than peace. She is officially considered the world's outstanding atomic target. Britain fully appreciates that if America retrenches on her foreign policy, an atomic attack could easily come from elsewhere. Thus America, despite her politics, is looked upon here as the armor against aggressors and as a peaceful partner. The Russians, with their current program, can never hope to crack the pedestal of prestige upon which the British have placed us.

Nevertheless, the average Briton still thinks of the United States in terms of streamlined automobiles, luxurious apartments, five-pound steaks nibbled and discarded at every meal, wheat and potatoes ploughed under, big cigars lit by dollar bills, gold pieces used as paper weights, and juke boxes playing singing commercials.

[2] Report from David Schoenbrun, CBS correspondent in Paris.

Occasionally, ideas of the American scene penetrate this fog of inaccuracy. Thus it is recognized that we have a form of culture of our own, that every American is not a millionaire, that some of the gold stored in Kentucky is British, that we ship great quantities of food abroad.[3]

A poll taken by *Time,* Inc., in Europe in March 1948, adds more details to this picture. People in five European countries were asked a number of questions designed to bring out their attitudes toward the United States. When asked, "If you were to leave home, what country would you like best to live in?" Swedes and Italians showed marked preference for the United States. The French, who on the whole are pretty well satisfied to stay in France, slightly preferred life in Switzerland over life in the United States. The English put the United States in fourth place, after Australia, South Africa and Canada. Germans thought the United States by far the best place for businessmen, farmers and workers to make a living.

The same poll sought the Europeans' estimates of America's motives in the Marshall Plan. The results (more than one answer was given by many of those interviewed) were these:[4]

	Britain	France	Switz.	Italy	Ger.	Sweden
			(Percentages)			
Prevent Communism	49	64	64	70	80	62
Anxious to help Europe	33	16	30	26	44	46
Wants allies in Europe	31	38	21	40	29	31
Get rid of goods	14	26	21	14	25	20
Force way into markets	10	13	20	23	9	12
Impose capitalism	8	14	6	11	3	9

This poll is evidence that there is a basic body of opinion in Europe that can be won to our side, if we make ourselves understood—and provided always that the economic picture improves.

[3] Report from Merrill Mueller of NBC.
[4] "Where Stands Freedom?", A Report on the Findings of an International Survey of Public Opinion, conducted by Elmo Roper for *Time,* February-March, 1948.

When we compare European attitudes toward the United States at the beginning of 1949 with the situation a year or two ago we find there has been a turn in our favor. There has been a growing feeling that our aid is not only an attempt to establish a bulwark in Western and Central Europe against the advance of Soviet Russia, but also that it stems from a desire to put Europe back on strong economic and political foundations.

The desire for closer bonds and understanding with this country arises in part from the increasing fear of Soviet Russia. The methods of Moscow, and of Moscow's followers, remind Europeans of Hitler's behavior. Suppression, in the Russian-dominated areas of Eastern Europe of those who oppose the Communists has put fear into European hearts. The surly actions of Messrs. Molotov and Vishinsky at international conferences have aroused grave suspicions. And the measures taken by Communists against church and property have made many men and women in Western countries look upon Communism as a scourge.

The fight on the Marshall Plan opened many European eyes to the full meaning of the Communist strategy. The tired peoples of Europe—and they include not only the peoples of Western Europe, but also the peoples of the Russian satellite nations—eagerly welcomed the aid that might restore normal life, but they soon discovered that the Communists, under orders from Moscow, were trying to sabotage it, and their resentment flared up.

The Communists, as a result, suffered a moral defeat in the cold war. They also have suffered a material defeat. For Russia has been unable to supply goods to Western Europe and to those satellite countries which had been forced to forego altogether Marshall Plan aid. Communist ideology has been unable to take the place of American goods.

Nevertheless, we must not be misled. Admiration for our strength, need for goods and raw materials from the great American storehouse are not synonymous with respect for our social and political institutions, nor for our way of life. And it is necessary that we achieve this deeper understanding of the United States if we are to win the psychological battle with Soviet Russia.

3. *The Communist Propaganda Method*

Soviet propaganda in Russia and throughout the world is directed by the Agitation and Propaganda Committee of the Central Committee of the Communist Party. The importance of propaganda in the Soviet scheme is demonstrated by the fact that both external and internal propaganda is supervised by members of the Politburo. Every form of expression—newspapers, radio, magazines, music, books, political talks—is considered part of the propaganda apparatus. Inside Russia alone more than a million persons are involved in propaganda work.

With this mighty weapon, Moscow is trying to convince the workers, the peasants and the intellectuals of the rightness of the Communist cause and the wrongness and selfishness of American policy. There are four main lines in the Soviet propaganda attack: first, that the United States is now the great threat to the world; second, that the capitalist system, of which we are the high priests, is doomed; third, that the United States is headed hell-bent toward a bottomless depression; fourth, that ours is not a united nation but two Americas, consisting of a ruling class and a serf class.

Numerous variations are played on these themes. They are introduced and withdrawn as circumstances and opportunism dictate. Within Russia itself the Soviet press and radio maintain a barrage of half myths about the United States and Britain. They emphasize the plight of the Negro in the United States. They spread the idea that there is a great mass movement of the underprivileged, peace-loving people who are held down by the industrialists, militarists and financiers through their twin instruments, the Democratic and Republican parties. The British worker is pictured as worse off under the Labor Government than ever before; he is characterized as a tool of Washington.

Soviet propaganda is elastic. When directed at particular peoples it has particular things to say, such as:

To Germans: It is the West, not Russia, which is determined to partition Germany; and the United States is seeking to create in Germany a market where it can sell dear and buy cheap.

To the British: By following the leadership of Washington and New York, England is being led inevitably into war.

To the French: Involvement with the Anglo-American "war-mongers" entails rearmament and saddles French taxpayers with needless expenditures.

To the Greeks: The civil war is prolonged not by the northern neighbors of Greece, but by American intervention. The only hope for peace lies in repudiating the West and entering the Soviet orbit.

This propaganda barrage is laid down by many weapons and with great intensity. For example, at the beginning of 1949 the Soviet radio was broadcasting 210 hours weekly by short wave to the rest of Europe. And the Russian satellite countries, carrying the same themes as the master Moscow radio, were broadcasting 234 hours weekly in various languages to the rest of Europe. These broadcasts from Radio Moscow; the broadcasts of the little Radio Moscows in Prague, Belgrade, Warsaw, Sofia and Bucharest; the articles and reports appearing in *Pravda* and *Izvestia* and in the little *Pravdas* and little *Izvestias* in the satellite countries; the editorials and reports in the Communist newspapers and magazines published in Paris, London and in other Western cities; the Communist books and pamphlets —all flow together into a mighty river of distorted information and plain misinformation, channeled so as to submerge all opinion favorable to the United States.

A brief survey of the Communist operation in occupied

Germany throws light on the propaganda approach elsewhere in Europe. The cost of Moscow's propaganda in Germany is estimated at $75,000,000 annually. This propaganda is wrapped around a central idea: the German people are warned, with a side glance at the mighty Russian army on their frontiers and with a few reminders of what that army recently did in Germany, that their future depends on Russia.

The main channel of Soviet propaganda in Germany is the Political Department of the Soviet Military Administration, at Karlshorst in the Soviet sector of Berlin, which employs a small army of workers, German and Russian.

The Russian Military Government, by a system of licenses, gives the Soviet propaganda organization power of life and death over every radio station, newspaper, publishing house, political party and cultural institution in the Russian zone of Germany and in the Russian sector of Berlin.

The Soviet-controlled press in Germany is the most important weapon in the Communist arsenal. Of the twenty newspapers now published in Berlin, ten are Soviet-licensed. Their daily circulation is 850,000 in Berlin, but larger in the Soviet zone, as compared with 1,350,000 for the ten papers licensed in the British, French and American sectors of Berlin. In the Soviet zone of Germany the Russians have licensed approximately 37 newspapers sponsored by the Communist SED (Socialist Unity Party). The Western powers have difficulty in supplying newsprint, but the Russians, with rich supplies originating in their zone, can afford to be generous. The Communist papers receive twenty times more newsprint than the non-Communist.

The Russians exercise outright control of the only two wire services permitted in their zone—the SNB (Soviet News Bureau) and the ADN (General German News Bureau). SNB frequently marks important items, important to Soviet policy, with the word "Pflichtmeldung"—meaning "it must be published." Other items are designated "desirable." German editors of the Soviet-licensed press say they are frequently called to task by the Russian control authorities for failing to carry the necessary quota of SNB items. Obviously, most editors must comply. Obviously, criticism of Communism or of the Soviet Union is not tolerated.

Public speeches are another important method of indoctrinating the German people. The Moscow-trained party leaders of the SED operate several Karl Marx schools in the Russian zone. Carefully selected Germans from all four zones attend these schools. They graduate as trained agitators ready to carry the party line to lecture platforms, public assemblies, farms and factories. Theaters and movie houses, as well as schools and universities, in the Russian zone are parts of this propaganda net.

This survey of the Kremlin's propaganda indicates something of the power and complexity of the attack being made on us. Crusading under the banner of Communism, and using every type of weapon, Moscow and its followers are laying down a concentrated barrage on our ideological position.

4. *The Challenge We Face*

Many theories have been advanced as to the best method of meeting the Communist challenge. There are those who think that the story of American business achievement is the most effective answer in Europe to the charges made by the Communists. One American observer in Central Europe has summed up this argument by saying that "the best possible American propaganda in Europe would be the free and wide distribution of the Sears-Roebuck catalogue."

There are sound reasons for rejecting this theory. American goods are important in the psychological struggle in Europe. But there is something equally important to be put into this battle. That is the idea of American democracy itself. We may well keep before us these words of Professor D. W. Brogan of Cambridge University:

Poor relations may respect the family millionaire and may be grateful for his aid, but the mere example of his wealth does not necessarily endear him to them—especially if they don't understand him any too well. That is why many Europeans do not regard the United States with unalloyed enthusiasm. Their respect for America's power is, let us admit it, tinged with envy and criticism. Because of certain extravagancies and follies in American life—and because America has not taken the trouble to explain the real sources of its strength to Europeans—they are apt to say that luck is the reason for America's present position.

... Riches are a great reality and the world is too poor to despise them or even plausibly to pretend to despise them. But they are not all the strength of America, of the country of Lincoln as well as of Ford. And the best and most effective Americans have always remembered that even more than riches, righteousness exalteth a nation. That is true and never more true than in an age where moral foundations have been shaken and the pursuit of mere power and mere efficiency has led to the bunker in the chancellery and the ruin of a nation, which next to America, had most "know-how" and most belief that the machine and industry could do all things.

It is therefore important for both Americans and Europeans to understand that the key to America's power lies in qualities which derive from the social and political soil of the United States. For it is these qualities, rather than material power as such, that point the way to Europe's salvation.[5]

Our propaganda, to be successful, must have a spiritual as well as a material content. It must feed people's minds as well as their bodies.

In communicating the American message we have two main channels of approach. The first is governmental—through official agencies such as the Voice of America and through diplomatic representatives. The second approach is by American private enterprise—through American news agencies, newspapers, magazines and films circulating in Europe.

Individually and teamed together, these two play, or can

[5] The *New York Times Magazine,* November 14, 1948.

play, a vital role in meeting the challenge. In the next three chapters the role of the two forces and their successes and failures in Europe are described.

CHAPTER EIGHT

VOICES OF AMERICA

By W. Phillips Davison

THE CONFUSIONS that can result from the failure to evaluate properly the word "propaganda"[1] are revealed sharply when we begin consideration of the State Department's public opinion operation overseas. There are still gaping differences of opinion as to what the government's role should be and, as a result, a number of theories as to what the government should do—theories that very often contradict one another in whole or in part. In the main these theories can be classified in five categories:

1. That we should give people abroad the facts about us. This may be called the "fair trial," or "cross section of America," theory. It assumes that once people have the facts, they cannot fail to approve of us and to concur with our policies.

2. That we should bring people abroad to understand our objectives. The assumption here is that comprehension of American cultural ideals and achievements will break down anti-American prejudice.

3. That we should persuade people abroad to like us. Here we cross the narrow line that separates information from propaganda. Our purpose becomes to display as in a show window those aspects of American life calculated to arouse a favorable response abroad: the best American music, American generosity, American peacefulness.

4. That we should induce people abroad to favor the

[1] See Chapter One, pp. 12-14.

democratic way of life and to reject totalitarian philosophies, especially Communism. This means combating the information or propaganda programs of other countries.

5. That we should induce people abroad to favor specific items of American foreign policy. If pushed to the limit, this may amount to psychological warfare.

Statements by Department officials before Congress, or to the public, have usually emphasized (1) the information or (2) the cultural approach, or a combination of the two. For example, Dean Acheson, then Under-Secretary, told a House of Representatives sub-committee in May 1947:

A great deal of misguided, misleading, and I think foolish talk which has gone on at some times, to the effect that the purposes of the United States are imperialistic or reactionary, or militaristic, would be utterly impossible in any part of the world which clearly understood what kind of people the American people are and what they are doing.[2]

And Secretary Marshall, emphasizing understanding more strongly, told a Senate committee in July of the same year:

There is no question today that the policies and actions of the United States are often misunderstood and misrepresented abroad. The facts about the United States are withheld or falsified and our motives are distorted. Our actions do not always speak for themselves unless the people of other countries have some understanding of the peaceful intention of our people. An understanding of our motives and our institutions can come only from a knowledge of the political principles which our history and traditions have evolved, and of daily life in the United States.[3]

More recent official statements have tended to stress the necessity of combating the information programs of other countries. Secretary Marshall, appearing before a House Appropriations sub-committee early in 1948, said:

It is a tragic fact that many people in the world today live in

[2] Hearings, U. S. Information and Educational Exchange Act of 1947, House, May 13-20, 1947, p. 9.
[3] Hearings, U. S. Information and Educational Act of 1947, Senate, July 2-5, 1947, p. 24.

areas where only the air is free. All they know about the intentions and motives of the United States is what they are told through a completely controlled press and radio. As you know, our international efforts are daily subjected to distortion and falsification. The State Department has not had the means to counteract this campaign effectively. We now ask that this arm of the Department be fully strengthened, especially as it has been accorded formal legislative status.[4]

In their day-to-day operations Department officials, particularly those in the lower echelons, usually have in mind objectives (3), (4) and (5)—the strictly propaganda phases. Some officials engaged in foreign radio broadcasting have come to regard their activities as a duel with Russian publicists and policy makers. Others, occupied with the formulation of high policy, stress the winning of the minds of those who dwell in what we have called the gray areas, the debatable ground between the spheres of influence of the United States and the Soviet Union.

This failure to agree on an exact definition of our task abroad must be kept constantly in mind when we survey the problems and the performance of the State Department's assignment overseas.

The official chiefly responsible for public opinion operations abroad is the Assistant Secretary of State for Public Affairs (who is also in charge of most of the Department's domestic public opinion operations). He functions through the Office of International Information and the Office of Educational Exchange which, through various divisions, direct the Voice of America, supply news reports and pictures to foreign publications, provide educational movie shorts for overseas distribution, stock American libraries and information centers in foreign cities, arrange for the exchange of students and professors and conduct other cultural and educational activities. The actual overseas work of these offices is handled by the United States Information Service, which

[4] Hearings, Department of State Appropriation Bill for 1949, House, p.
[5] See Chapter One, pp. 36-37.

is organized under the various embassies in foreign countries. USIS gets its material through the divisions under the Assistant Secretary for Public Affairs, but its personnel are responsible directly to the ambassador or minister in each country and therefore are outside the jurisdiction of the Assistant Secretary. As in the domestic field, the public opinion operation abroad is two-fold: First, there are the *intelligence functions* and, second, there are the *information-propaganda functions*.[6]

1: *The Intelligence Functions*

The State Department's methods of determining public opinion abroad are not nearly so well organized as those at home; for example, there is no branch in the foreign operation comparable to the Division of Public Studies, which tries to analyze domestic public opinion and to delineate the areas of ignorance. Instead, the Department is dependent upon the staffs of the embassies and legations.

The political reports of the ambassadors and ministers themselves often contain information that is valuable in determining public opinion policy. Moreover, the public affairs officials attached to our embassies and legations have some intelligence functions; in an informal way they have a responsibility to study public opinion and to make recommendations through the ambassador. These intelligence methods are extremely haphazard. As a result there are large gaps in our information about the people we are trying to inform and to influence. The effectiveness of the operation suffers accordingly.

But the defects in the intelligence operation are not confined to the gathering of information. Many of the reports received from our diplomatic representatives abroad may contain intelligence that could be of great value in the opinion field, but too often these reports do not get to the desks of the officials concerned with the information-propaganda

[6] See Chart B on next page.

Chart B

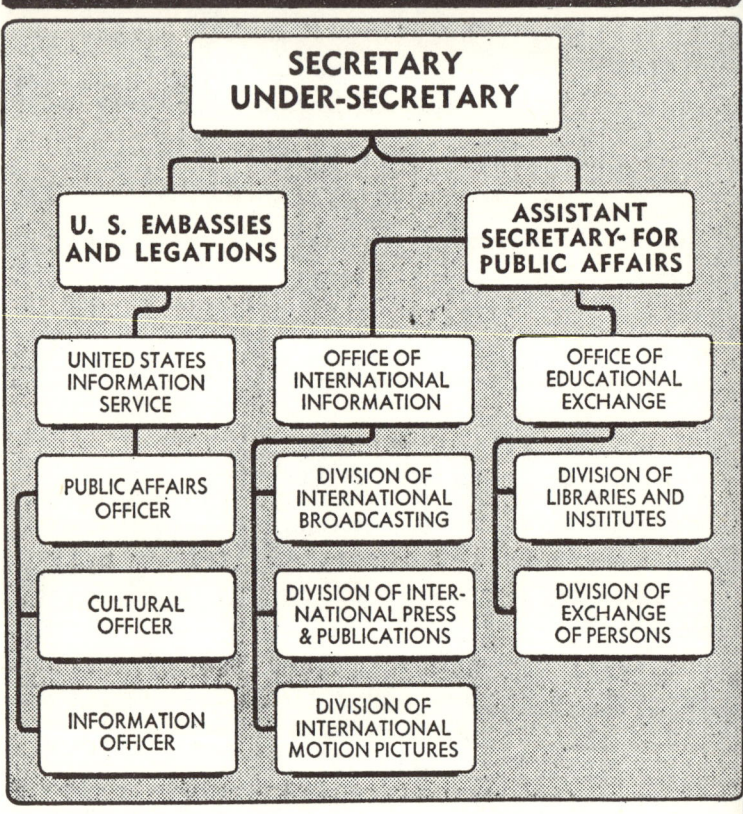

(This is the set-up as of January 20, 1949. Some structural changes were then expected with the advent of Secretary Acheson.)

THE SECRETARY AND UNDER-SECRETARY set the broad lines of policy of our intelligence and information-propaganda programs abroad.

ASSISTANT SECRETARY FOR PUBLIC AFFAIRS is concerned primarily with information and propaganda in the foreign operation. His functions are carried out through two Offices with five subsidiary divisions:

OFFICE OF INTERNATIONAL INFORMATION directs and coordinates the activities of these three divisions:

(Continued on bottom of next page.)

job. They go to the State Department's Planning Board and to one or two top officials. As a result very often the Office of International Information's appraisal of public opinion in a given country is based on the personal opinion of a program director in New York, plus what he reads in the morning newspapers. In contrast to our method the British have a policy of sending all but the most confidential diplomatic reports to the information officers.

Obviously these methods—of getting intelligence and of using it—are far from adequate if our overseas information-intelligence program is to be effective. Not only must we get

---

(*Continued from bottom of preceding page.*)

Division of International Broadcasting which directs the Voice of America, the State Department's radio operation.

Division of International Press and Publications which supplies news reports and pictures to foreign publications.

Division of International Motion Pictures which provides educational movie shorts for overseas distribution.

OFFICE OF INFORMATION AND EDUCATIONAL EXCHANGE sends to and receives from other nations information in economic, social, educational, technical, scientific and cultural fields through these two divisions:

Division of Libraries and Institutes provides books and other cultural materials for libraries, cultural centers, schools, or other institutions in foreign lands.

Division of Exchange of Persons arranges exchanges of students, professors, specialists and other persons who wish to obtain experience.

U. S. EMBASSIES AND LEGATIONS try to keep foreign peoples informed about us and channel intelligence about foreign public opinion to the State Department.

UNITED STATES INFORMATION SERVICE is the division of the embassies that handles personal contacts with foreign newspapers, motion picture theaters and other media, and distributes material prepared by Office of International Information.

Public Affairs Officer directs the work of the Cultural Officer and Information Officer; has informal duty of studying public opinion and making recommendations through the diplomatic representative.

Cultural Officer assists ranking officers in cultural matters and keeps State Department informed of local developments in cultural fields.

Information Officer maintains liaison with foreign newspapers and magazines and keeps them supplied with American news and photographs.

better and more detailed information about the people overseas, but we must see that that intelligence is taken fully into consideration in shaping our information-propaganda program.

2. *The Information-Propaganda Functions*

The information-propaganda program falls into three general categories: (a) the Voice of America, (b) the direct activities of USIS, and (c) the long-range cultural operations in which USIS also plays a big part.

a. *The Voice of America*

The Voice of America is the State Department's radio operation. It is directed by the Division of International Broadcasting from offices on Fifty-seventh Street in New York City. Every day the Broadcasting Division's short-wave transmitters beam programs in twenty-two languages to foreign countries.

Through arrangements with foreign stations the Voice of America is also heard overseas over medium- or long-wave transmission. This is made possible by three devices.

In many countries the programs are picked up and re-broadcast over local stations. The British Broadcasting Corporation picks up and re-broadcasts to Europe programs totaling several hours daily, in German, Bulgarian, Czech, English, French, Greek, Hungarian, Rumanian, Slovene and others. In Austria and Germany local networks also re-broadcast programs aimed at those countries. The official French radio uses a 30-minute State Department program each day. In addition, various stations in Italy, China and Korea relay our broadcasts. The State Department also uses short-wave relays in Munich and Honolulu, and has others under construction. These provide clearer short-wave signals than could be produced from any point within the United States.

A second device which brings American programs to foreign listeners consists in the distribution over local stations of program scripts and transcriptions. The foreign broadcasting division sends musical recordings to approximately 75 stations throughout the world. The division also supplies more than 30 stations with recorded spoken material. In addition, it sends scripts in English, French, German, Italian, Polish, Portuguese and Spanish to State Department offices in 35 foreign countries for local distribution. (Local radio stations, it should be noted, requested this type of material from our embassies and legations long before it was available.)

A third device, less frequently used but still important, is the production of programs over foreign stations by the Department's information officials. The State Department radio officer in Paris, for example, has produced as many as five programs a month over the French radio, in cooperation with local radio authorities. Moreover, information personnel abroad are frequently able to get their short-wave and re-broadcast schedules listed in locally published radio magazines; failing this, they often advertise them in State Department news releases on public bulletin boards.

Broadcasts to different countries vary widely in content, but all include fairly complete news coverage. The State Department must rely for its news reports on the International News Service, Reuters, Aneta and other smaller wire agencies. (The Associated Press and the United Press have refused to sell or give their reports to the State Department because they say they do not want to take part in a "propaganda program.") From the available sources, there is prepared a file of the principal news of the day; it is circulated to the radio language desks, which select items of greatest interest to their several areas. Sometimes the various desks explain news items in some detail to fit the requirements of the particular audiences in question. In totalitarian countries, for instance, listeners find it difficult to understand why the American Congress is so slow at arriving at decisions;

why, after the President has recommended a program, it may take several months before the program is put into effect. With this in mind the State Department has prepared numerous scripts that explain the operation of our system, the tradition of unlimited debate in the Senate, and the procedure of exhaustive committee hearings.

Special feature programs are also broadcast to most areas. These may consist of interviews with Congressmen of both parties, talks by high government officials, round-table conferences of experts, travelogue descriptions of the United States, book reviews, dramatizations of current events, and descriptions of life in the United States. During a recent two-month period, twenty-four special features were prepared on newly published books, eight describing conditions in various states of the Union, and three on business and industry.

The finest music produced in the United States is beamed to other parts of the world and is simultaneously recorded for distribution abroad. Musical programs have included performances of the Metropolitan Opera and of symphony orchestras and concerts of American artists, as well as folk music. These programs, in addition to entertainment, tell the story of American accomplishment in the field of music.

Nobody knows exactly how many people listen to the State Department's foreign broadcasts, nor even how many foreigners have short-wave receivers. It has been estimated, however, that in the areas at which the programs are beamed 30,000,000 sets are capable of receiving them. This estimate is necessarily very rough; also, the condition and the range of the sets are not known.

Scattered information regarding the size and composition of the State Department's audience may be gathered from letters received from listeners, from occasional public opinion polls, from reports from United States missions, and from the reactions of foreign officials and media. None of this information, however, tells how individuals abroad hear the programs, whether direct via short wave, or through rebroadcasts or re-programming over local stations, nor does it often make clear what effect the American programs have on the attitudes and opinions of foreign listeners.

During 1946, the foreign broadcasting division received over 50,000 communications from listeners all over the world; of these, approximately 65 percent came from Europe, 25 percent from Latin America and 10 percent from the Far East. In 1947 listener mail increased to almost 150,000 pieces; it has since decreased considerably, largely because the personnel necessary to reply to listener mail were eliminated by a budget cut in 1947. The listeners request program schedules and scripts, they comment on the programs and ask the innumerable questions and request the favors with which all radio stations and publications are familiar. Taking into account the difficulty of obtaining writing materials in many parts of the world, and the cost of overseas postage, this volume of mail appears to indicate a substantial and interested audience.

Two public opinion polls may be cited as illustrating the listening habits of foreign peoples. Between November 1 and 4, 1946, the Hungarian Public Opinion Research Service, at the instance of the State Department, conducted the last survey the Department has been able to obtain from behind the Iron Curtain. About 2,000 out of approximately 100,000 radio subscribers in Greater Budapest were interviewed. Of all those questioned, 62 percent, 1,240 persons, said they could receive foreign broadcasts on their radios. These 1,240 persons were classified by the Research Service according to social groups as follows:

	Intellectuals	Bourgeois (percent)	Workers
Usually listen to London	68.4	45.5	59.4
Usually listen to New York[7]	32.5	28.7	35.5
Usually listen to Moscow	22.3	21.9	25.7

[7] At the time this poll was taken it is believed that an American-operated Austrian station was transmitting a daily program in Hungarian, which lis-

A substantial number of the respondents said that they listened to broadcasts in the English language. Their reasons for doing so were: desire to learn the language, more interesting programs, better receiving conditions, and more convenient times of broadcast. A smaller number also listened to State Department programs in German and French.

During the Summer of 1948 American Military Government made a survey of radio listening habits among the residents of the western sectors of Berlin. Over 40 percent of all adults in this population said they listened to the radio fairly regularly, and of those 7 out of 10 heard Voice of America broadcasts.

Surveys to determine the number of listeners in France, Italy, Sweden and Finland are currently under way.

Several American diplomats have pointed out that in countries where newspapers and the radio are rigidly censored, although only a small percentage of the population can hear short-wave broadcasts, news spreads rapidly by word of mouth. Maynard B. Barnes, former U. S. political representative in Bulgaria, reported:

Perhaps only 5 per cent of the rural population actually individually listens to a radio. That 5 per cent listens every evening at 6:15 to the Voice of America and goes out to the pubs in the course of the evening and recounts what the Voice of America said.[8]

W. Averell Harriman, former Ambassador to Russia, made a similar observation before a Congressional committee in 1947. He said:

One must realize that when there is a controlled press and controlled sources of information, that people look for any scraps of information from abroad, and when anybody gets a scrap of information from abroad, the circulation of the knowledge from mouth to mouth is amazingly fast and extensive.[9]

---

teners may have confused with programs originating in New York. Some respondents gave more than one answer.

[8] Hearings, U. S. Information and Educational Exchange Act, Senate, 1947, *op. cit.*, p. 54.

[9] Hearings, U. S. Information and Educational Exchange Act of 1947, House, *op. cit.*, p. 32.

The same conclusions were reached by those who studied listening habits in Germany during the Nazi régime. Information obtained from broadcasts by a small number of persons received a far wider circulation by word of mouth than would have been likely in a country without censorship. In this respect, the effectiveness of broadcasts received from abroad may prove greater in a totalitarian state than in a democracy.

Finally, reactions in the Russian belt give some indication that the Department's broadcasts are having effect. Each Communist attack on America's "propaganda broadcasts" is a sign that the material is finding an audience. These attacks are frequent in the broadcasts of Moscow and the satellite countries. They indicate that the Russians are sensitive to what the Voice of America is saying and also that Russia believes it has to counter the Voice's statements. Recently, Hungarians listening to the Voice of America have been harassed by the Communist-controlled police of that country, on the charge of "inciting against Hungarian democracy."

Many valid criticisms are made of the Voice of America. Some grow out of the failure of the State Department to determine exactly what it wants its propaganda agencies to say, and out of its failure to supply the broadcasting division with up-to-date reports and interpretations of developments as they occur. Others are the result of lack of imagination and planning in the broadcasting division, and of Congress' failure to provide adequate funds for a first-rate operation. What follows is an evaluation of the most important points made by the critics.

Lack of direction. Today's radio operation is an outgrowth of the wartime Voice of America conducted by the Office of War Information. In O.W.I. days the guide lines for policy were fairly clear: "Broadcast anything that will help win the war." Now the waters of policy are muddy; clearly defined objectives are lacking. Consequently, the

Voice of America is frequently slow in interpreting important developments.

More than any other division of the State Department, the foreign broadcasting division feels that it is a stepchild, often abandoned to grope its way in the dark. The division is seldom briefed in advance by policy makers in the Department. Frequently it gets no briefing at all even after the announcement or event.

This lack of policy direction puts the Voice of America at a great tactical disadvantage vis-à-vis its chief competitor—the Russian radio. Radio Moscow often beats it by hours—and sometimes days—presenting the Russian point of view while the American broadcasters are waiting for a directive.

Program content. The Voice of America programs are frequently dull. The interpretations of events—even when there is no lack of directive from Washington—often indicate a fundamental misunderstanding of people and events. Moreover there is much criticism that full use is not made of the dramatic possibilities of radio—good dramatizations, good actors, humor. Finally, the Voice of America often seems unaware that there are differences in the tastes of the countries to which we broadcast.

Technical deficiencies. Even if its policy were clear-cut and its programs sparkling, the Voice of America would still be badly handicapped by technical difficulties. Short-wave signals are difficult to pick up, and the reception is often marred by static. If the programs are to reach a maximum audience, the medium- and long-wave re-broadcast arrangements with foreign countries should be greatly expanded.

Many of these criticisms arise out of circumstances over which the Division of International Broadcasting has no control. In many cases its deficiencies are due to the fact that it does not have the funds to recruit and hold the staff required to do an adequate job. Not one of its twenty-two language desks is adequately staffed. The Voice of America to Greece, for instance, has been one writer-translator-announcer who puts on a fifteen-minute news broadcast. Information officials recognize the need for improving programs to Greece, but their chief worry is that the Voice to Greece will come down with the flu.

Conditions such as these can be remedied only by Congress. Yet in Congress there remains considerable suspicion of the whole broadcasting operation. The tendency of American politicians to misinterpret what the foreign broadcasting division is trying to accomplish periodically throws the division into a turmoil. The badly overworked personnel of the foreign language desks occasionally make mistakes—sometimes small errors of judgment and sometimes more egregious boners. Congressmen have seized upon some of them, inflating them into momentous issues. An example is provided by the famous "Wallace broadcast" in the Spring of 1947, in which the State Department shortwaved a review of Russell Lord's *The Wallaces of Iowa* to Germany and Austria. Henry Wallace was then in Europe, making speeches which were decidedly in opposition to State Department policy. A factual review of the book was given in some 600 words. Furthermore, the review, for the benefit of Germans who had been impressed with Wallace's speeches, quoted the following excerpt:

> Whenever the members of this family turned to agriculture and its problems, their achievements were considerable. When they turned to other problems, the success was dubious.[10]

Various Congressmen heard about the broadcast, but had no clear idea of its content. They telephoned the State Department for information. The Department could not help them because the script of the broadcast was in New York. Furthermore, it had been written in German, and had not yet been translated. Hence, the principal criti-

---

[10] Translated from German broadcast, "What America Is Reading," April 23, 1947, as quoted in the *New York Times,* April 4, 1947.

cisms of this broadcast were made without knowledge of its contents, and many of the misapprehensions regarding it were never adequately corrected. The State Department, it is true, should have had better information about the material broadcast over its facilities. But with limited personnel, it is hard to see how it could have done much better in this case. The public criticism of this broadcast was followed by the resignations of two of the most able German-speaking personnel who had shared responsibility for producing it in the New York office; it proved impossible to replace them.

Moreover, some of the deficiencies in the Voice of America broadcasts have been due directly to the fact that it has obeyed Congressional orders. For example, in 1947 the Congress ordered the Voice of America to "farm out" 75 percent of its overseas programs to privately owned networks. The preparation and transmission of the programs were assigned to the networks under nominal State Department supervision. In practice, the broadcasting division rarely saw the scripts. This situation led to extreme embarrassment in the Spring of 1948 when a furor arose over a series of broadcasts, prepared by one of the radio networks under contract and transmitted to Latin America, which described in humorous vein various states of the Union. Senators seized upon such statements as:

> Nevada has no interest itself—it's a land of cowboys, and its two principal cities are in competition. In Las Vegas people get married and in Reno they get divorced.

and described them as "damnable lies," "downright falsehoods" and "pure drivel." [11]

The furor resulted in the cancellation of the outside contracts by the Voice of America and centralization of operational responsibility for all broadcasts in the State Depart-

---

[11] *New York Times*, May 27, 1948.

ment. But the incident built new obstacles for the Voice of America in getting adequate appropriations for its operation.

The foregoing leads to the inescapable conclusion that not all the faults of the Voice of America are of its own making. Obviously the policy makers of the State Department as well as the law makers in Congress must take a more sympathetic and understanding view of official radio propaganda. Then —and only then—can the Voice of America play its full and proper role in bringing foreigners to understand and accept our policies.

b. *The United States Information Service*

The radio is only a part—although a big part—of the government's overseas operation. Equally important, in the view of many observers, is the task of dealing directly with foreign peoples through their newspapers, motion picture theaters and other media. This job of personal contact and distribution is handled by the United States Information Service attached to the American embassies and legations. Each USIS office is headed by a Public Affairs Officer who reports to the U. S. ambassador or minister. Under the Public Affairs Officer are several other officials concerned with information. Their exact number depends on the size of the office, but among them usually are an information attaché, a cultural attaché, a press officer, a film officer, a student exchange officer, a librarian and sometimes a radio officer. These are the officials whose daily work brings them into contact with foreign newspapers, magazines, educators, students and film audiences, and on whom the success or failure of our foreign information program largely depends.

In the USIS operation, foreign publications are regarded as of first importance. Every day a file of approximately 7,500 words of news material prepared in Washington is sent by Morse code to 57 American diplomatic posts throughout the world. Another 150 posts, which do not have monitoring facilities, receive the material by air mail. This news file, known as the State Department *Wireless Bulletin,* in most cases is translated at the receiving end where it is furnished to local newspapers, magazines, and other interested organizations or individuals. The *Bulletin* does not cover all events but places emphasis rather on complete texts of official statements, summaries of government reports, detailed accounts of Congressional hearings, and other types of authoritative information which commercial news services usually find too expensive to send overseas in full. Such material is indispensable to foreigners who wish to gain an accurate picture of American foreign policy; it serves as background information for editorial writers, speakers and teachers and provides text for front-page reports. An *Air Bulletin* is also sent to the Department's offices abroad by air mail.

Feature material and photographs supplement the *Bulletins*. Stories about life in the United States, often accompanied by photographs, are used by the press in many countries. These stories may be of a general nature, describing farming in the Middle West, for example, or they may deal with specialized topics such as the buying power of the dollar. Film strips—a series of still pictures which can be shown successively with a projector—are also dispatched to our representatives abroad, who in turn supply them to lecturers and teachers.

The news and photographic material dispatched to foreign countries by the Department is used, according to official estimates, by more than 6,000 newspapers and magazines in almost every country of the world. During the fiscal year 1947, 23 missions (less than half of those receiving the material) reported that they had placed 5,221 items a month from the *Wireless Bulletin* and 5,815 documentary articles a month in local publications having a total circulation well over 100 million. Even behind the Iron Curtain, cultural and other non-political articles and pictures achieve considerable circulation.

Deserving of special mention is the Russian-language magazine *Amerika*. Prepared and printed in this country, this magazine gives a well balanced picture of American life. The monthly issues include profusely illustrated articles on such subjects as the life of the auto worker and American literature. While the number of copies sold, 50,000 a month, is small in view of Russia's enormous population, the number of readers per copy is believed to be very large; individual pages, even, have been found on sale in black markets.

Motion pictures provide a third medium through which the State Department communicates with mass audiences abroad. This work is supervised by the Division of International Motion Pictures of the Office of International Information. The Division distributes no commercial motion pictures, only educational and non-theatrical films, most of which it obtains from other governmental agencies, from commercial companies which have prepared films on subjects of interest to their publics, and from private foundations. The subject matter of the small number of films produced especially for the foreign information program is varied, for example the scenery of the United States, hygienic methods of preparing food, soil conservation, epidemic control, the operation of American schools, and the functioning of American government. These educational films are assembled in Washington and dispatched to our diplomatic missions overseas, where they are shown before groups which request them and lent to individuals who wish to show them privately. The State Department has estimated that approximately six million persons per month attend the showings, and considers that the possibilities for increasing this number are very good.

The effectiveness of USIS operation abroad is difficult to gauge. Although much of its press material is used, there is no way of telling how lasting is the impression made. Reports received from correspondents overseas[12] are critical of many aspects of the program, but none of them suggests that the program should be dropped. On the contrary they are in agreement that it should be improved and expanded.

One frequent criticism is that the USIS staff is too small and, in many cases, too unskilled in information work to do an adequate job. Nearly all the correspondents agree that the success or failure of the Department's efforts in any country depends not so much on the material it sends from Washington, although of course this is important, as on the number and quality of the Americans in charge of the information and cultural program in foreign capitals. The pay-off is abroad. British propaganda, it is pointed out, is more effective than American because British information and cultural officers make a point of becoming acquainted with leading writers, educators and political figures in the countries where they are stationed. American press attachés are held in low esteem by many overseas newsmen, being characterized as the "cast-offs of the foreign service" and "bureaucrats," and USIS personnel are rated only somewhat higher.

c. *The Cultural Agencies*

The Voice of America and the information activities of the USIS offices abroad can go a long way toward keeping foreign people informed about United States policy and the way it fits into world affairs, but to bring about a deeper understanding of American life and culture more intensive efforts are needed. We must make provision for ample background information and we must also try to build in foreign countries a corps of specialists who can help explain the United States to their fellow citizens. Libraries and educational opportunities are the two principal means which are being used to attain these ends.

[12] The group referred to on p. x.

Within the State Department in Washington the Division of International Libraries and Institutes and the Division of International Exchange of Persons (both parts of the Office of Educational Exchange) are responsible for directing these phases of the program. They procure books, teaching aids and other materials in the United States for shipment to our USIS offices abroad, and they also enlist the cooperation of numerous American cultural agencies as a means of furthering their educational task.

Libraries and information centers, and the arrangements for the exchange of students, professors, artists and technicians, exercise a more gradual—and possibly deeper—effect on the attitude of foreigners toward the United States than do the mass media. Not primarily concerned with current American policy, the libraries and educational exchange are helping to build up a reservoir of understanding and good will which in the long run will exercise a permanently beneficial effect on international relations and on American prestige abroad.

The State Department maintains 53 libraries throughout the world and 28 Inter-American Cultural Centers, with 22 branches, in Latin America. The Information Libraries are staffed and maintained directly by the Department through the USIS offices, but the Cultural Centers are now self-supporting and administered by locally constituted bodies of North Americans and Latin Americans. These institutions all maintain reading rooms stocked with American magazines and newspapers and most of them have collections of American books.

About 4,000,000 readers use the libraries every year. Their influence is far greater than the number of readers indicates, for those who turn to the libraries for information are usually persons of some influence in the community—people who are leaders of opinion. A record of one month's telephone inquiries received at the United States Library in London, for example, disclosed that 30 percent of the calls came from newspapers and magazines, almost as many from business firms, and over 20 percent from professional men and scientific workers. The librarian in Bangkok has reported that most frequent users are local government officials, followed by business firms, professional people and journalists.

When in 1947 budget cuts forced many American libraries throughout the world to close their doors, the resulting protest made it clear that these institutions were filling a real need. An editorial in *Die Burger,* an Afrikaans daily, observed when the library in Capetown, South Africa, was closed:

Die Burger's readers were more indebted to the service of the libraries than they realized. The information service was of valuable assistance to the press and other institutions in South Africa. It kept us informed about American affairs more completely than any news service could, and the libraries were the embodiment of the best American conceptions of efficiency and service.

The Office of Educational Exchange maintains contact with American-sponsored schools, libraries and cultural institutions throughout the world, assisting many of them to obtain teaching materials, reference books, or scientific equipment. To some it has given financial grants. Observers abroad agree almost unanimously that these institutions, particularly in the Near East, have been influential in promoting good will toward the United States and understanding of the American point of view.

Finally, the State Department promotes the exchange of cultural emissaries in modest fashion. Within the United States the Department helps private organizations engaged in the exchange of persons for educational, cultural or good will purposes. For example, when lack of shipping threatened to prevent large numbers of American students from carrying out plans to study in Europe during the Summer of 1947, the Department arranged with the United States

Maritime Commission for the use of two ships. The Departments acts as intermediary between associations in the United States and similar groups abroad and has helped several hundred American business firms in arranging exchanges of personnel with foreign firms for educational purposes.

In addition, the Department on its own initiative arranges exchanges of students, professors and those who wish to obtain experience in foreign countries. During the fiscal year 1947, the Department provided financial aid for almost 400 foreign students and professors to enable them to study in the United States, and aided approximately 100 United States students, professors and technicians who wanted to study in the other American republics. More important than direct financial aid is the activity of the Department as a catalytic agent, stimulating and facilitating exchanges which are actually carried out by private organizations and institutions. Latin American students in the United States in 1947 numbered more than 3,000; of these more than half had been given some type of assistance or advice either by the Department in Washington or by its cultural and information officers stationed abroad. Students from countries outside Latin America, now coming to the United States at the rate of approximately 15,000 a year, receive many non-financial services from the Department, from its representatives abroad, and from private American organizations under contractual arrangements.

All these cultural activities are essentially long range in character. Their effectiveness cannot be measured in terms of the day-to-day propaganda war. Among the correspondents queried overseas there was considerable difference of opinion about them. One correspondent describes them as "mildly inoffensive." But another writes: "The children who throng the USIS library in Cairo will probably remember and respect the United States much longer than any older person reading a press release in his morning paper."

3. Some Suggested Improvements

The foregoing pages have stressed two kinds of improvements needed in the State Department's foreign public opinion program. There are, first, the factors which Congress controls, and, second, the factors which the State Department itself can control.

With regard to factors in the first category, it is obvious that the sums which Congress has thus far appropriated are wholly inadequate. Recruiting capable personnel, however, depends only in part on having more money to spend for salaries. Government service will never be able to compete with business on a purely monetary basis. Only by offering positions that seem to give opportunity for important public service will the Department be able to attract the kind of men it needs. At present, it must be admitted, those opportunities are not apparent, for neither Congress nor the American public has shown very high esteem for the foreign information and cultural activities of the Department of State. For example, when the Marshall plan was set up, Congress, because of its great distrust of the State Department, virtually instructed ECA officials to have as little truck as possible with the Department. As a result, ECA has set up an information service of its own; it cooperates in a way with USIS (which is an instrument of the State Department) but to too great a degree it operates independently in the information field.

With regard to the factors which the State Department can control, there is much that can be done. It is true that the State Department's foreign venture is new, and on that account both the public and its representatives in Washington have been suspicious and hostile, perhaps stupidly so. But it is also true that obvious defects in the Department's program have given ground for doubt and hesitancy, if not for active opposition.

The State Department does not at present define the purposes of its activities with respect to foreign public opinion, and it will be unable to do so until the opinion operation has been integrated into the business of policy making. Foreign public opinion cannot be influenced appreciably by a program which lacks clearly defined objectives, or which suffers from internal conflicts. Only through basic agreement on objectives and coordination of mechanisms can the full impact of modern public opinion techniques be brought into play to win men's minds to the American point of view.

CHAPTER NINE

ASSIGNMENT FOR THE PRESS

By C. D. Jackson

AMERICAN MOVIES are seen by millions of Europeans. News gathered by American wire services is printed in many hundreds of European newspapers. American newspapers, magazines and books are on sale in most European countries.

All this adds up to a vast amount of American private activity in Europe that affects public opinion, particularly the opinions of many Europeans who are not reached by our official propaganda. Although this activity is privately financed it is a fundamental part, in some countries the most important part, of the whole complex of activities which can help to make Americans better understood abroad.

In this book it has already been argued—and, it is hoped, demonstrated—that in the cold war of words all our deeds abroad, all our writings, all our publications, all our expressions of thought must be weighed according to their propaganda impact. That is why all private activities affecting public opinion abroad have, in effect, a propaganda aspect, using the word without an invidious sense and in its true meaning.[1] That is why in the Economic Recovery Plan specific provision was made for helping to promote the circulation of American publications and American ideas in Europe.

Because of this propaganda aspect, private activity affecting public opinion abroad places a large responsibility on those who conduct it. They can do much to create an honest and helpful impression of America, or, by misusing

[1] See Chapter One, p. 17.

their opportunity, they can do great harm to America's world position and to America's foreign policy—and thus to their own enterprises.

The operations abroad of American private industry in the information field can be grouped in four major categories: (1) press services, (2) newspapers and periodicals, (3) motion pictures, and (4) books.

This chapter is an attempt to analyze for each category the extent of the activity, its effectiveness and the possibilities of an increase in effectiveness. The facts given and the conclusions reached are drawn from original research, from the reports of the thirty-four correspondents who contributed to these studies[2] and from the writer's experiences and observations in the field.

1. *Press Services*

To understand the activities of the American press associations in Europe we must consider the newspapers which they serve, either directly or through sale of their services to the various central news agencies. European newspapers, suffering from severe newsprint restrictions, bear little resemblance to the newspapers of the United States. They rarely exceed ten pages and usually consist of four to six. Compared with our own papers they carry little advertising. With the exception of a few outstanding newspapers published in England and on the Continent, they are mainly party journals, more often devoted to editorializing than to printing the news. Many of them run the less responsible members of the American press a close race in playing up "yellow news."

There has been an extraordinary post-war increase in the number of European newspapers which get their news from the three major American news services—the Associated Press, the United Press and the International News Service. In 1939 the AP had just begun to break into the overseas

[2] See p. x.

news market; today it serves 1,493 newspapers and radio stations outside the continental United States, of which 469 are in Europe. The UP during the same period increased the number of overseas customers which it serves directly from 485 to 1,058. INS enlarged the number of its overseas clients, from 100 to 495. Competition among the services for these foreign customers is keen.

The American associations send out daily news reports somewhat similar in content to their reports for domestic papers, but generally with special emphasis on news of interest to the foreign market. In their foreign operations the associations are confronted with two special problems: (a) Too often the more serious dispatches about American events and American policies are side-tracked by foreign editors in favor of sensational material—stories about Hollywood divorces, gangland murders and the like. (b) In countries behind the Iron Curtain there is much evidence that the reports are distorted in the interest of Communist propaganda.

With regard to the selection of sensational items by European editors, the associations are in a difficult position. In the domestic field they operate on the principle that the news agency supplies the reports and the rest is up to the newspaper editors. This principle often results in distorted emphasis in the domestic press, but the distortion is mitigated by the variety of news media available to the American public. In the foreign field, however, the facilities for correcting distortions do not exist, and therefore the problem is much more complex. Thus there is indicated a large task of education, the task of convincing foreign editors and foreign readers of the importance of having the kind of news service that will give them a true picture of America. Obviously, this is a long-term assignment.

But time presses and, therefore, such short-term measures as can be adopted must be adopted without delay. The news agencies should examine their overseas operations with extreme care because of their great importance in the psychological struggle. There have been charges that they are not doing the fully effective job that is needed. They might well put to themselves questions such as these: Is our foreign service too sensational? Do we give it the attention it deserves? Do we man it properly at home and watch it carefully abroad?

With regard to the deliberate distortion of news in Communist countries, that is a more delicate problem. The American news services have contracts to supply news reports to countries behind the Iron Curtain. The question is raised as to whether or not these contracts are detrimental to our interests. It is not a new problem, even though it has never before existed in its present intense form. Writing seven years ago of his long campaign against control of news sources and outlets by the old Reuter agency, Kent Cooper, general manager of the Associated Press, said:

> In the . . . postwar era a free press and freedom of international news exchange everywhere must be guaranteed. There can be no permanent peace unless men of all lands can have truthful, unbiased news of each other which shall be freely available at the source to all who seek it there, wherever that may be. The flow of news must not be impeded. Those whose business it is to get the news at the source must be under no restraint or dictation by governments. This can come to pass only when, as to news collection, all the barriers are down.[3]

These words are more meaningful today than ever before; their implementation, however, presents many difficulties. For example, the Associated Press has made a series of short-term experimental agreements with the central news agencies (that is, the official government agencies) of the countries behind the Iron Curtain—Russia, Czechoslovakia, Poland, Hungary, Rumania and Yugoslavia. Under the agreements, the AP report is supplied to these agencies on the condition that they do not change the facts or the mean-

---

[3] Kent Cooper, *Barriers Down*, New York, Farrar & Rinehart, 1942, p. 9.

ing of what they receive. AP correspondents stationed in these countries are expected to observe and report on material used under these agreements. But such inspection is difficult; it requires a great deal of time and diligence; often misrepresentation is accomplished by selection and emphasis, rather than distortion of facts.

One thing is certain, that the Communist agencies operate on the theory that theirs is a propaganda job and a service to the state, and their aim is not the objective presentation of the news which is the goal of the true American newspaper. In Communist countries the official propaganda offices are in direct charge of the press, and the distortion is dictated from above. The ethical question is raised: Should the wire services sell news reports when they know those reports are going to be twisted to misrepresent American life?

On the affirmative side there is the argument that if the American news agencies refuse to sell to Communist countries, they will deprive the readers in those areas of any chance of getting anything in the nature of a fair report; by sending the report there is always the chance that some favorable news may trickle through. On the negative side there is the argument that the news agencies, by permitting their reports to be used for Communist propaganda purposes, are lending the prestige of the American news-gathering organizations to Communist purposes.

2. *Newspapers and Periodicals*

American newspapers and periodicals distributed abroad are read by a relatively small but influential audience. Some are English-language publications which are circulated chiefly among government officials, civil servants, professors, teachers, journalists, business men and students. Others are published in various foreign languages and have a greater mass potentiality.

Many of the American newspapers and periodicals read abroad are printed abroad. A number of United States publishers have established branch publishing offices overseas, both to print and to distribute their publications.

The *New York Herald Tribune,* daily European Edition (English language), printed in Paris, has a circulation of 63,000 [4] in Western Europe, Germany and Austria, the Middle East and North Africa.

During the United Nations sessions in Paris last fall the *New York Times* began distribution of a special air-mail edition overseas—an edition composed and printed in New York and flown overseas for distribution within twenty-four hours of publication. It also prints an Overseas Weekly (English language) which has a total circulation of 24,000 (in Germany 10,000).[4]

The *Rome American,* an English-language daily published in Rome, is distributed principally in Italy, Greece, Saudi Arabia, with token distribution elsewhere in Europe. Circulation is approximately 25,000.

The *Reader's Digest* has done the most extensive job in overseas publishing. Starting before the war with an English edition printed in Britain, on V-J Day it was putting out editions in Spanish, Portuguese, Arabic (since discontinued), Swedish, Finnish, Danish and Norwegian. Since 1945 it has added Japanese and French, plus two more English editions for Australia and South Africa, a Canadian edition (in English and French) and an edition in German. The combined circulation of all these editions totals 4,275,000.

Newsweek prints two special English-language editions abroad, one in Paris (circulation 44,519 [4]) for Europe and Africa, the other in Tokyo (circulation 26,221 [4]) for the Pacific area.

Time International English-language editions include

---

[4] Includes circulation among U. S. military personnel as well as among foreign civilians.

Canadian and Latin American publications, an edition printed in Tokyo and Honolulu for Asia and the Pacific, and an edition printed in Paris for Europe, Africa and the Middle East. Combined circulation: 261,546.

Life International (English language), published fortnightly in the United States for distribution abroad, has a circulation of 252,082.

McGraw-Hill translates four of its trade publications into Spanish for Latin American audiences: *El Automovil Americana* (16,000), *El Farmaceutico* (8,000), *Ingenieria Internacional Construccion* (9,000), *Ingenieria Internacional Industria* (11,000). It also puts out three international editions in English: *The American Automobile Overseas* (10,000), *Pharmacy International* (2,700), *McGraw-Hill Digest* (15,000).

Several other Spanish-language magazines are published in the United States for Latin America; among them are *La Hacienda* (circulation 25,884), *Norte Revista Continental* (circulation 126,095) and *Cine-Mundial* (circulation 55,000).

Another group of magazine publishers has engaged in international publishing to the extent of turning over to local publishers in various countries the reprint rights to their magazines, either in the original English or for translation into the language of the country. Such locally reprinted United States magazines include *Omnibook, Magazine Digest,* and some of the Macfadden and Fawcett publications.

A third group of publishers regards the foreign market simply as an extension of its domestic market, exporting copies of its regular United States editions for limited subscription and newsstand sale abroad. The major firms in this group are Curtis Publishing Company, Crowell-Collier, Look and Hearst International.

A fourth group of publishers, mostly comic book and pulp-fiction concerns, looks on the foreign market as a dumping ground for surplus or unsold newsstand copies left over from its domestic distribution. Before the war there was a substantial demand for these surpluses in the English-speaking countries. The demand presumably is still there but those countries, along with many others, have passed, or are about to pass, laws prohibiting the "dumping" on their markets of second-hand or back-date foreign magazines.

The American publishers who print abroad pay their printing costs in local currencies, but their paper is dollar-purchased and shipped, their editorial content is dollar-created, and their American personnel abroad are dollar-paid. Almost all circulation income, and part of advertising income, is received in local currency which foreign governments are generally reluctant or unable to convert into dollars. Because of this economic disadvantage, provision was made by Congress to permit the exchange of a limited amount of Marshall Plan dollars for such blocked currencies.[5] This established one of the links between government and private enterprises in the overseas operation.

It should be recognized that there are certain American publications circulated abroad that do not contribute to a proper understanding of America. Some are guilty of sensationalism and distortion. Some elaborate on phases of American life or politics that tend to diminish our prestige in Europe. Some carry across the seas the personal axes they grind at home; thus they give the European reader a one-sided view of controversies that he cannot understand without a knowledge of American politics or business. Still others—and not only the comic book publishers—look upon Europe as a dumping ground for their surplus material without regard to the impression that material may create. Obviously this kind of journalism benefits neither the nation nor, in the long run, the enterprises themselves.

[5] The first agreements under this provision were announced in December 1948.

3. Motion Pictures

More people see American films in Europe and in the rest of the world than at home. Eric Johnston, President of the Motion Picture Association of America and of the Motion Picture Export Association, estimates the foreign audience for American films at 110,000,000 weekly, the domestic audience at 90,000,000. Movie houses all the way across Europe, including Russia, depend on the American product. British theaters, for example, require about 350 new feature pictures a year, but Britain's film industry produces only 50 or 60. In France 60 percent of all films shown are American; in Belgium about 70 percent. Even in Soviet Russia, *Pravda* recently felt it necessary to castigate the provincial movie theaters for giving more time to old American pictures than to new Soviet films. American films—with foreign-language subtitles—reach large numbers of Europeans who cannot or do not read American newspapers or periodicals. Thus the motion picture has a strong propaganda impact.

The foreign market is an economic necessity to Hollywood. Film costs are so geared that sales overseas provide the entire margin of profit for the industry. In the post-war years this income has been hard hit by the dollar shortage abroad and by restrictions imposed in many countries on the import of American films. Consequently, competition for the foreign market is keener than ever among the major studios.

Most American films distributed abroad are produced by the ten leading film companies which are members of the Motion Picture Export Association.[6] There are a few independents in the field, but their share of new films for the foreign market is less than 9 percent of the total.

[6] Allied Artists, Columbia, Loew's, Paramount, RKO, Twentieth Century-Fox, United Artists, Universal-International, Warner Brothers and Republic Pictures. All these except United Artists are also members of the Motion Picture Association.

The foreign market for American films falls into two categories. First, there are the countries—embracing 90 percent of the overseas market—where there is, in theory at least, an open market, although there may be commercial restrictions limiting the number of film imports. Second, there are the countries—embracing about 10 percent of the market—where either military occupation authorities or Communist governments operate as distribution monopolies for all motion pictures; they are Germany, Austria, Japan, Korea, Indonesia, the Soviet Union, Poland, Czechoslovakia, Yugoslavia, Hungary, Rumania and Bulgaria. In all these countries importers of American films must deal either with military authorities or with Iron Curtain film monopolies.

In countries in the first category film exporters operate on their own. They have their own agents overseas and arrange for their own distribution on a competitive basis. What quotas there are, are set by the importing countries. For example, France recently limited imports of American films to 121 a year; other foreign films to 65. In dividing the American quota, the French Government assigned eleven licenses each to the ten members of MPA. The other ten were assigned to non-member producers.

Although the Motion Picture Association of America has no control over the pictures its members send to these countries, the member companies do more than 90 percent of the export business. They receive guidance from the Association's Selectivity Department, whose job it is to "review all films contemplated for export and to advise the exporting company as to their suitability for release in various countries." Films are classified as "Group I—suitable; Group II—not advisable; and Group III—unsuitable." Two members of the Selectivity Department operating in Hollywood study scripts before and during production and suggest changes designed to improve the export suitability rating.

The Selectivity Department has no set code by which it

judges pictures or scripts. Its objective is to eliminate objectionable elements from a picture during production or to persuade a member company not to ship overseas a completed picture "which might be detrimental to the prestige of the United States if released abroad." For example, the Selectivity Department of the Association would not approve for export a motion picture which contained a sequence holding up to ridicule or contempt the electoral process in the U.S.A. The department may adjudge a picture "suitable" for some countries but "unsuitable" for others. It might find, for example, that English-speaking nations have the necessary background for a certain film but that the same film would mislead Slavic countries as to American institutions. But, in any event, the department's recommendations are not binding; the final decision is up to the distributor.

To deal with countries in the second category MPA in 1946 set up the Motion Picture Export Association (MPEA). In the occupied countries, all films selected by MPEA must have the approval of the occupying authorities. In the Iron Curtain countries MPEA follows this procedure: It selects a predetermined number of titles from its stockpile of several thousand unreleased features and offers them as a block to the film monopoly which contracts to take a given number from the list offered. For example, Poland in 1947-48 contracted for 65 films selected from a list of 100; Czechoslovakia bought 80 selected from a list of 120; last fall Mr. Johnston closed a deal with the Soviet Union under which Russia agreed to buy 20 films from a list of 100; Yugoslavia agreed to take 25 from the same list.

In preparing these lists the Export Association has a relatively free hand since all its member companies divide the receipts of the Export Association on a predetermined basis and therefore are not interested in pressing for selection of their own pictures as against a competitor's. With several thousand films to choose from and 350-450 additional pictures added to its available product annually, the officers of the Export Association first prepare a basic release list containing films of various types—musicals, comedies, action pictures, romances, dramas, etc. The basic schedule is submitted to the MPA Selectivity Department which passes judgment on suitability or unsuitability of the list submitted. Here are some of the standards applied: "Does the picture in any way distort, exaggerate or mislead in its portrayal of Americans or the American way of life?" "Is there too much vice or violence in the picture?" "Would the film give serious offense to the governments or people of one or more MPEA territories?" "Will the film encounter serious cutting at the hands of local censor boards?"

Thus Hollywood does have the machinery for selection of "the best American films" for export. In practice, however, the MPA's Selectivity Department rates very few films as "unsuitable." MPA explains the low figure by the fact that objectionable features are generally eliminated on the Hollywood set. (MPEA of course discards many more because its foreign market is restricted.) Therefore, by Hollywood's standards, practically the entire production of MPA members is rated as "suitable" for foreign consumption.

There are many critics who do not go along with Hollywood on this. They contend that many Hollywood pictures create, and contribute to, distorted impressions of American life abroad; that there is considerable emphasis on the sensational aspects of the domestic scene; that the impression left with the foreign movie-goer—who cannot step out of a movie theater into the realities of American life—is one of an America hellbent for crime and fun in noisy and gaudy terms. These critics argue that there is no real selectivity practiced in Hollywood; that in effect "marketability" carries as much or more weight than "suitability" in the selection of export films.

Hollywood defends both its motives and the quality of its product. With regard to motives, Eric Johnston says, "Hollywood is acutely aware of its responsibility as the guardian of a great medium of mass communication. Its record in peace . . . will measure up to any other instrument of expression. . . . The average foreign movie-goer regards our pictures with respect because Hollywood has not tried to make it appear that American democracy is Utopia."

With regard to quality, Hollywood argues that the critics are misinformed. Examples such as the following are cited:

"Not long ago, some of our government and private critics were horrified because 'The Grapes of Wrath,' a picture based on the Steinbeck novel, was shown abroad. 'Too seamy!' they cried. 'That's a side of American life better untold outside our borders.'

"Yugoslavia pirated a print of the film and showed it under the title, 'The Paradise That Is America,' gleefully pointing to the plight of our migrant workers in the days of drought and depression as a typical, permanent American condition. The Communists thought they had a damning weapon against democracy in their hands.

"Our critics and the Communists were both wrong. The thing that impressed the Yugoslav audiences was that the migrant workers drove away in their own jalopies when the police chased them out of the tent-and-shanty town."

Again: " 'Ali Baba and the Forty Thieves' has been the most popular American film shown in Czechoslovakia, running for nearly six months in Prague. The Czechs found great satisfaction in this legend where the heavy-handed dictator is eventually overthrown by the common people."

The examples are interesting. There are other films that have been good propaganda. For example, in the Italian elections in the Spring of 1948, American films were extremely effective.[7] There is a widespread feeling, however,

---

[7] See Chapter Ten, 199-200.

that such films are in the minority—in short that Hollywood is not doing the job it could do in explaining America to Europeans.

4. Books

American books, sold abroad either in the original or in translation, are highly influential in intellectual circles. American novels are widely read. American scientific works are in great demand because of America's preeminence in scientific fields.

Before World War II American book publishers, entirely wrapped up in promoting and developing their domestic market, were not at all export-conscious. Not more than 2 percent of their total book output went abroad. Britain and France at that time were exporting between 30 and 40 percent of their production; they regarded the overseas book trade as an instrument of foreign policy.

During the war American book publishers, working with OWI, furnished a vast quantity of books to liberated countries, an activity which stimulated them to give serious thought to post-war possibilities. In October 1945, they combined their efforts in the foreign field by forming as a "chosen instrument" a non-profit corporation, the United States International Book Association.

With a membership that eventually included 124 publishers (among them all the leaders in the industry), with the blessings of the State Department and with $125,000 of government money, USIBA set out to follow in the footsteps of OWI. Its announced purpose was to make United States books "freely and economically available throughout the world, and make the best products of our technology, education, culture and entertainment at least as fully known and easily available abroad as the books of any other nationality."

USIBA set up book centers in foreign capitals, organized

book fairs and traveling book exhibitions in several countries, arranged for short-wave broadcasting of reviews of American books, distributed a monthly book list abroad, and compiled a definitive bibliography of scientific, medical and technical books. These activities attracted much attention to American books, and contributed in large measure to the $2,000,000 sales handled by USIBA during its first year of existence.

Originally set up as a two-year experiment, USIBA was hitting its stride after this first year, but then its members came to a parting of the ways and decided to go back to operating abroad on the old every-man-for-himself basis.

In 1947, despite the demise of USIBA and the continuance of foreign exchange restrictions, officially reported exports of American books to all countries showed a substantial gain over 1946, from $18,700,000 to $24,000,000. The 1947 exports were almost five times what the Department of Commerce reported in 1938.[8] If mail shipments had been included, the 1947 total would have been increased to approximately $50,000,000. Comparing this figure with an estimated 1947 book production of $352,000,000, we get an export quota of 15 percent.

The breakdown of 1947 exports by geographic areas, however, shows that only a relatively small proportion of the American books sold abroad go to the areas where the cold war is being fought most bitterly. Of the officially reported exports in 1947 amounting to $24,000,000, sales valued at $7,700,000 were made to Canada. Only 28 per-

---

[8] Yearly exports as reported by the U. S. Department of Commerce, *not including mail shipments*, were:

	To Canada	To all countries
1938	$2,130,476	$ 5,219,314
1944	5,009,350	8,676,382
1945	5,762,525	11,605,243
1946	7,644,416	19,406,101
1947	9,701,363	24,294,851

cent ($6,889,000) went to Europe. European sales were distributed as follows:

	Dollar volume	Percent of total
Western Europe	$6,033,511	24.8
Germany[9]	56,579	.2
Russian satellite countries	319,840	1.3
Russia	252,450	.1

The exports of American books to overseas markets in 1948 declined about 20 percent from 1947 total. The United States Department of Commerce estimates the dollar volume of sales abroad last year at approximately $19,000,000. The prospect for a reversal of this downward trend in book distribution abroad is not regarded as good so long as the present restrictions on dollar exchange obtain in most of the countries of the world.

The question here, as with the other media of the press, is whether the book industry should not realize the importance of the contribution it could make to the job abroad and, accordingly, again set up an organization, a "chosen instrument," to do that job.

5. The Basic Issue

In all four fields—news agencies, newspapers and magazines, motion pictures, and books—the basic issue is the same. It is the issue of whether those who control these media will recognize and assume their responsibility abroad.

Even though it has been said before in this book, it should be said again: that the American press when it operates abroad is in effect doing a propaganda job, as well as undertaking a commercial venture; that there is too little appreciation of the fact that Europe is an ideological battleground.

---

[9] The German figures do not include American books distributed through such governmental agencies as the Department of the Army, the Department of State and the Library of Congress. For the fiscal year 1948, $785,000 was allotted to the Department of the Army for the purchase of American books.

Private information organizations should not see Paris in terms of Chicago, or Rome in terms of New York. Once they leave our shores, our newspapers, magazines and films are more than newspapers, magazines and films; they are representatives of America.

Private enterprise should develop an increased awareness of its international responsibility, an awareness that would result in better news, better movies, better books in Europe. And it must jealously guard against distortion.

Finally, the efforts of private enterprise should complement the government's efforts—and *vice versa*. Only this kind of teamwork can wipe out the areas of ignorance abroad about American ways, American motives and American policy—and, unless they are wiped out, our whole program will be injured immeasurably.

CHAPTER TEN

TWO VITAL CASE HISTORIES

By Arnaldo Cortesi and "Observer"

IN THE THREE preceding chapters we have discussed the job confronting us abroad and the roles of the State Department and private enterprise in carrying out that job. Now let us look at the principal battleground, Europe, to try to gauge how effective our program has been in the three major propaganda areas—the *black,* the *white* and the *gray*.[1] Are we or the Russians winning the battle for men's minds?

The Black Areas. These are the areas under complete or almost complete Communist domination. The channels of communication are largely in the hands of the Communists. Thus, we operate at a disadvantage; our program cannot be decisive in any immediate struggle. In these countries the reports indicate that, while the Russians are making full use of their advantages in communications, there is, in some countries at least, a strong residue of pro-American sentiment.[2] The Voice of America is the principal American propaganda weapon. If only because of the multiplicity of their media and their absolute control of governments, the Russians have the advantage.

The White Areas. These are the countries, England, for example, where the struggle between Communism and the West is not immediately acute. In them there is a strong popular sentiment for the Western way of life and there is no sizable Communist party to contend with. In them the

[1] See Chapter One, p. 36.
[2] See Chapter Seven.

propaganda job is now essentially one for private enterprise; our government's role is confined largely to cultural and educational affairs in order to build lasting good will. Here the Russians have made no gains; indeed, their policy and propaganda seem certainly to have increased dislike for the Kremlin.

The Gray Areas. These are the countries where the struggle with Communism is white hot and where the issue is gravely in doubt. The two countries most directly affected are Italy and France where there are strong native Communist parties and a fertile soil of unrest and economic instability for them to work in. In the Spring of 1948 in Italy one of the most important propaganda battles of the cold war was fought. In the year of 1949 in France an intense and perhaps decisive battle is being fought. Here are reports by special correspondents from the two countries. The report from Italy is a case history of the marshaling of propaganda weapons for a particular target. The report from France is an appraisal of the weapons and strength of both sides in the struggle now going on.

1. *Report from Italy—by Arnaldo Cortesi*[3]

This is an account of the propaganda battle that preceded the Italian election on April 18 and 19, 1948. At the beginning of the campaign, few people thought that the Communist-led Popular Front would obtain less than 40 percent or so of the total vote, and the extreme left-wing parties were supremely confident that they would exceed that figure by a comfortable margin. Step by step as the anti-Communist parties developed their campaign, in which American propaganda played a not inconsiderable part, the Popular Front's stock sank readily. When all the votes were in, it was found that the Popular Front's share was only about 31 percent.

It would, therefore, appear that propaganda (used in its

[3] Mr. Cortesi is the chief correspondent of the *New York Times* in Italy.

widest sense to include all the means and devices used by the United States, the Vatican and Italian anti-Communist parties, organizations and groups to lay their case before the voters) succeeded in detaching about 10 percent of the Italian voters from the extreme left-wing parties. The credit does not, of course, belong wholly—perhaps not even principally—to American propaganda, though it undeniably made its influence felt very strongly. Due credit must be given also to the unexpectedly efficient efforts of the Catholic clergy and lay organizations (especially Catholic Action and the Civil Committees) and of all the anti-Communist parties, among which the Christian Democrats occupy a dominant position.

The American propaganda effort was accompanied by certain moves in the field of international politics that without any question won many votes for the anti-Communist side. Noteworthy among these were the tripartite step for the restitution of Trieste to Italy and the discussion at the United Nations of Italy's application for membership. Both helped to put Russia in a bad light.

A powerful electoral device was also the thousands of letters written by Italo-Americans to their relatives and friends in Italy, urging them to vote against the Communists. These letters convinced many Italians of the unwisdom of throwing the Marshall Plan overboard by voting in a Communist government.

The anti-Communist campaign was waged through many media: films, radio, leaflets and pamphlets, the press, exhibits and speeches.

Films. The ten leading American distributors pooled their resources and distributed each other's documentaries, as well as American government documentaries, on a nonprofit basis along with their own films. At the same time, the Italian documentary companies produced three films on the effect of American aid to Italy and the leading Italian newsreel company, INCOM (Industrie Corti Metraggi), distributed several films on the same subject. This was done in accordance with the provisions of the Post-UNRRA Aid Bill, which specified that the Italian government was to take the necessary measures to inform the Italian people of the provenance of the aid they were receiving. It is calculated that the American documentaries were seen by five million people each week, and the INCOM shorts by eight million. All this was, of course, in addition to the normal distribution by United States Information Service of documentary films to political groups, parochial groups, scientific institutions, clubs, and the like. Six hundred thousand persons saw such films in the month before the election.

Special mention must be made of the film *Ninotchka*,[4] which appeared on Italian screens shortly before the election and made a deep impression everywhere. Double the usual number of copies were made of this film, and it was, by special arrangement, shown immediately in the houses that cater to the humbler sections of the population. Its effectiveness is proved by the fact that the Communists made several attempts to interfere with the exhibition of *Ninotchka* and that the managers of more than one movie theater were threatened with bodily harm if they did not take it off their programs immediately.

Radio. Most foreign programs relayed over the Italian networks were discontinued during the pre-electoral period, only those of a purely non-political character being left. Nevertheless, American short-wave broadcasts succeeded in putting on a few shows aimed at convincing the Italian voters of the interest and sympathy with which the people in America were watching developments in their country. One of the few foreign programs carried by the Italian stations was a one-hour show from Hollywood put on the air

[4] *Ninotchka* was a 1939 Metro-Goldwyn-Mayer film, starring Greta Garbo and Melvyn Douglas. It sharply and hilariously satirized life in Russia and, in general, it left the audience with a feeling that if this was Russia they did not want to have anything to do with it.

as part of a drive to raise funds for the orphans of Italian pilots who fell in the war. Many outstanding personalities of the movie world participated in it.

Leaflets and Booklets. USIS supplied the information on which several booklets and leaflets, issued by political groups and commercial editorial firms, were based. In the case of at least two booklets, the number distributed ran into the millions. Many copies were sent to working-class people by mail, and many more were distributed in offices, shops and factories, by Italian agencies and political groups. An example of the booklets was one entitled: *Cosa e' il Piano Marshall? Come il Ministero degli Esteri degli Stati Uniti risponde al pubblico.* (What is the Marshall Plan? How the Foreign Ministry of the United States replies to the public.) It was a translation of "Current developments report on European Recovery," No. 3, issued by the Office of Public Affairs of the Department of State. Another example of the booklets based on information supplied by USIS and distributed through Italian channels was one entitled: *Gli aiuti dell'America all'Italia. In che cose consistono? Sono indispensabili? Come ci vengono dati?* (American aid to Italy. What does it consist of? Is it indispensable? How is it given to us?) An example of the booklets issued by Italian editorial firms was one consisting of 64 pages and 37 illustrations, entitled: *Piano di ricostruzione Europea. Che cosa significa per l'Italia il Piano Marshall.* (European Reconstruction Plan. What the Marshall Plan means to Italy.) This booklet was put on sale at the price of 100 lire (about 17 cents), but thousands of copies were distributed free of charge.

Press. USIS kept a steady stream of information flowing to editors, writers, commentators, lecturers, parties, groups —indeed to anyone and everyone who asked for it. The technique followed was the one that has been shown to be best in practice, namely, to "make the Italians say it."

Many speeches by anti-Communist candidates were based on information supplied by USIS. Additional information was poured out through the daily Bulletin.

Exhibits. Exhibits entitled "The Worker in America," showing how working-class families live in the United States, were organized by USIS in Rome and other leading cities. They were invariably held in the poorer sections and were visited by many thousands of workers. The exhibits consisted of attractively presented photographs and statistics, and included also an hour and a half to two hours of documentary films dealing with labor questions, social improvements, labor-saving devices and the like.

Speeches. The speeches made by Ambassador James Clement Dunn did much to disseminate information about what the United States was doing for Italy. He delivered a total of about forty addresses after his arrival in Italy. Of particular importance were those he made at the arrival of the first, second and hundredth relief ship, and of each hundredth thereafter. The 600th arrived just before the election. The speeches were, as a rule, purely factual and emphasized the greatness of the effort that the United States was making to help Italy and the sacrifice that it cost the American people. A few of them also contained indirect, but unmistakable, warnings that American aid would cease if Italy were to go Communist.

It is difficult to assess the extent to which each form of propaganda contributed to the final result. Most authorities agree, however, that (apart from the tripartite step about Trieste, the discussion of Italy's admission to the United Nations, and the letters of Italo-Americans to people in Italy) films were by far the most effective form of propaganda. A man in very close touch with Communist Party headquarters, discussing the election results, said: "What licked us was *Ninotchka.*" He was exaggerating, of course, since *Ninotchka* was only the most notable of many films that made the Italian people weigh the comparative merits of a democratic and a Communist régime, but his statement nevertheless confirmed the importance of the movies in the electoral campaign.

Up to the time of the election campaign, American documentaries were shown only to restricted groups, while the ordinary run-of-the-mill commercial movies were often positively harmful from a propaganda point of view. But throughout the pre-electoral period the cooperation of the leading American distributors put films of positive propaganda value on virtually every Italian screen and so helped powerfully to save the day for the anti-Communist side. The success scored by the movies on this occasion suggests a new direction in which a continued American propaganda effort should work.

The extent of Russia's propaganda effort was more difficult to measure. The greater and most effective part of Russian propaganda during the campaign was indirect and carried on through the organs of the Italian Communist Party. It is therefore impossible to ascertain how much of the Communist propaganda had its origins in Moscow and how much in Italy. The poster war carried on by the extreme left-wing parties, for instance, was intense, especially in the early stages of the campaign, but there was little or nothing to indicate that the inspiration (as distinct from the money) for it was supplied by Moscow.

The belief that the Popular Front campaign was financed, at least in part, by Russia is based on inductive reasoning rather than on positive evidence. It is known that Russia sent some shipments of newsprint to the Italian Communist Party free of charge, but this was a mere fleabite compared to the cost of the whole campaign. No estimate of the total cost has been made, but 100 billion lire (over $150,000,000) is perhaps not exaggerated. The Popular Front is believed to have spent considerably more than all other parties combined, so that its share of the cost was far outside its financial possibilities, and it must have received help from abroad, or, in other words, from Russia.

The general impression in Italy is that the Popular Front spent its money unwisely. It was easily the first in the field and immediately began an exaggeratedly intense and costly campaign. The anti-Communist parties started late and remained a long way behind until the campaign was drawing to its close, when they gradually caught up with their adversaries and finally outstripped them. It is thought that the Communists (who were virtually footing the bill for the whole Popular Front) spent too much money at first and lacked the funds to react effectively at the end when the anti-Communist parties, and especially the Christian Democrats, put on their final spurt.

2. *Report from France—by "Observer"* [5]

The propaganda battle for France is being waged in a bitter atmosphere of almost pre-civil war tension.

The virulence and ferocity of the Communist effort strike the most casual observer. The tone of their press has never been more violent. Its principal targets are American imperialism and the Marshall Plan. They know that if American aid achieves its purpose their hopes in the West will be shattered.

What propaganda weapons are the Communists employing? Newspapers, posters, mass meetings, discussion groups, youth and feminist movements. The French radio, a state monopoly, is not at the disposition of the Party, although it is clear that some of the personnel are *noyautés* (fellow travelers).

The Communist press, generously supported by Party funds, served uncritically by Party writers, and its publica-

[5] "Observer" is an American newspaperman who has worked for many years in France. He has also engaged in information work abroad for the American Government.

tions tirelessly distributed (often gratis) by Party militants, is an instrument of primary importance.

L'Humanité, the four-page Communist daily, has one of the biggest circulations of any morning paper in Paris. It features front-page cartoons, scream headlines, violent editorials and shamelessly prefabricated news stories, in which bathetic sentimentality alternates with the most unscrupulous manhandling of facts. The paper sets forth the Party line in a language that is direct, brutal, inflammatory, that appeals to the tastes and prejudices of a working class audience. The only Communist evening sheet is *Ce Soir,* but it is pretty much of a loss, financially and otherwise.

Besides the two Paris dailies, the Party controls a number of provincial papers, strategically placed throughout the country, particularly in the industrial North and the traditionally Communist Midi.

The Communists also maintain a group of weeklies, each of which is definitely angled to hit one particular group: *Femmes Françaises* for the women; *La Vie Ouvrière* for the trade unionists of the Communist-dominated CGT (*Confédération Générale du Travail*); *La Terre* which, with a circulation of some 150,000, makes a bid for peasant support; and *Action,* a sheet designed for the intelligentsia. All of these papers are different in tone and approach, depending on the public to be reached. All handle the same themes, however, and at the same time. The directing hand of Moscow is only too clear in achieving this not-very-subtle orchestration.

The Communist press is dedicated to the principle that you can fool most of the people most of the time. Take their peasant publication, *La Terre.* While *L'Humanité* rages in Paris against the selfish farmers and the scandal of rocketing food costs, *La Terre* preaches a doctrine of agricultural subsidies that would warm the heart of the American farm bloc. *La Terre* is folksy and grass roots. No hint of proletarian struggle and despair here. It rages against the selfish manufacturers of agricultural machinery and protests against the high cost of fertilizer. In *La Terre,* Marxism seems closer to the *Country Gentleman* than to the urban proletariat.

In their French propaganda push, the Communists have the advantage of possessing experts with long experience in subversive activity. They draw financial support from Moscow. They have a stern, efficient discipline and a small, hard core of militants ready for any risk and any sacrifice. But they have been unable to win over the majority of the French people. They now realize that they can win France only through fomenting economic misery and political disorder—in a word, by sabotaging the Marshall Plan by every means at their disposal.

The Communist propagandists, it should be noted, have the advantage of a double status. They are French citizens and can speak to their fellows as such even though they owe their allegiance to a foreign power, and what they present as French opinion is in reality strictly dictated from Moscow.

Every loyal member of the Party is automatically an "information officer." Thus, the U.S.S.R. has at its disposition a propaganda outfit of several hundred thousand native Frenchmen who work as missionaries to spread Communist ideas among their friends, who can discuss politics with the habitués of the corner *bistro* with a naturalness that an American rarely acquires.

Each Sunday morning the streets of working class neighborhoods are spotted with young men and women hawking *L'Humanité.* Each neighborhood has its party center where official literature is disseminated, discussions held, strategy planned.

The only other group in France possessing something of Communist fire and fury are the Gaullists. But De Gaulle's propaganda resources are by no means so extensive as those of his Stalinist adversaries. It is well known that his RPF

(*Rassemblement du Peuple Français*) has its financial difficulties; it receives no considerable subventions from any known group or foreign government.

In comparison with the dogmatic assurance of the Communists and the Gaullists, the propaganda activities of the Socialists, the MRP (*Mouvement Républicain Populaire*) and other middle-of-the-road groups seem rather ineffective. There is no doubt that the French "man in the street" hopes for a moderate solution for the woes that beset him. What he wants more than anything is to be left alone to live and to work. He is curiously indifferent and even apathetic to what we consider the great issues of our time. He is not very keen on either Stalin or De Gaulle. But he is also uncomfortably convinced that moderation is not in the order of things.

Representatives of the U. S. Government and the American press—who regard the Communists as a far more dangerous foe than the Gaullists at present—are not taking the Communist propaganda push lying down. We are learning the score and putting up stiffening opposition to the Moscow-directed assault. But there are a number of important factors in the French situation which condition and sometimes handicap our effort.

From 1940-1944 the Nazis staged a massive, well-orchestrated, cleverly directed, lavishly expensive propaganda campaign to win over the French, whom they realistically recognized as the key nation in the "New Europe." The French eye, ear and conscience were incessantly bombarded by the full Nazi propaganda battery.

The net result is that the French are hyper-sensitive to any and all propaganda; they are opposed in principle to what they call *bourrage du crane*. *A priori,* they hesitate to believe anything they read in the papers (as far as the French press goes, you can't blame them), anything they hear on the radio, anything they see in the newsreels. In France we must combat, not simply an enemy propaganda, but a disbelief in the possibility of real communication, a corroding and all-pervasive skepticism which ultimately destroys the power to judge and to act.

Another difficulty we face in presenting our point of view is that we speak to the French as foreigners—even as the Germans did. The Leftist press, moreover, delights in pointing out that many of the Nazi slogans, such as "Defense of the West," "The Formation of European Union," etc., have now been Americanized. Moreover, Americans, working in an official position, never have the direct contacts with the working class which the Communists cultivate so assiduously.

And this is the class we must convince, the class which, up to the present, we have been least successful in convincing. As for the rest—the industrialists, the businessmen, the prosperous farmers, the economically sophisticated generally—we have them in the bag. Any textile manufacturer in the north whose mill is running full time, thanks to the cotton and the coal provided by the Marshall Plan, does not need to be convinced.

The economic and financial reviews, the serious newspapers like *Le Figaro,* willingly take our side. For all the middle and upper class, there is no question of choice. They are with us—and not simply from sentiment. They are very scared of the Russians. Their support is being forcefully and intelligently consolidated—and extended—by the present American information effort in France.

The Voice of America has a faithful audience in France. The United States Information Service performs a large number of important services: press, radio, motion pictures and graphics, cultural relations, liaison with the provinces. Its daily news bulletin, *USA,* goes out to all French newspapers and is widely used by practicing journalists. It plays a genuine opinion-forming role. A USIS library and reading room in its headquarters on the rue du Faubourg-Saint-Honoré offer a rich documentation on American questions. The library has an especially appreciated technical section where professional reviews and publications are available.

The provinces—which play such an important part in French life—are not neglected by the American information and propaganda effort. Regional offices of the USIS have been established in key cities such as Strasbourg, Lyons, Bordeaux, Marseille. USIS in Paris maintains liaison with them and provides them with printed materials, films, lecturers, etc.

The Marshall Plan mission to France maintains a small information staff of its own, which works in close cooperation with USIS. USIS facilities are used for the distribution of Marshall Plan publications, including a regular weekly bulletin sent to some 5,000 opinion-forming persons and groups (newspaper and magazine editors, prefects, Chambers of Commerce, labor leaders). A special effort is being made to establish strong bonds with non-Communist labor unions (*Force Ouvrière* and *Confédération Française des Travailleurs Chrétiens*), through the labor advisers and the labor information officers attached to each ECA mission. The American magazines and newspapers circulating in France contribute much to our total information effort. The vogue for things American has resulted in a considerable increase of persons reading and speaking English, notably among the middle classes.

None of these American publications, however, reaches the workers in the dreary stretches of the slums of Aubervilliers. It is only too clear that we must make a strong effort to win the sympathy of the workers. Speaking as representative of the American government, the American program cannot employ the polemical fury, the violence, the brutal manhandling of fact which is the stock in trade of its Communist adversaries in swaying labor opinion. So far, we have not been successful in speaking to the working man in his own language. For him the Americans are all of another class, of another world; they are *gosses des riches* whose sympathies go to the *gens bien* of the 16th *arrondissement*. To touch this popular group, it will be necessary to cut loose in our propaganda effort and move in with both fists flying. But whether this can be done while retaining official dignity and position, without frightening our more prosperous friends, is still another question.

* * *

These reports from the two crucial areas in Europe indicate the extent of our problem and what can be done. Although we won a battle in Italy, we have not won the war. In France the great tests lie ahead. The situation in both countries emphasizes this fundamental fact: If we are to win in Europe, we must engage in the ideological struggle as vigorously as do the Russians. We must make the working classes of both countries the main targets of our attack. In its way the propaganda program will be as important as the Marshall Plan itself in determining the outcome.

CONCLUSION

This chapter offers some recommendations designed to make the public opinion instrument more effective; it considers the complex question of leadership and opinion; and it concludes with a plea for a sound foreign policy—which means fundamentally a policy based on a sound public opinion.

CHAPTER ELEVEN

OPPORTUNITY OR DISASTER?

By Lester Markel

THIS IS THE insistent fact: that we have failed and are failing to give to public opinion the emphasis and direction it must have if it is to be the vital instrument we need.

These are the immediate results of that failure: that, at home, we are confronted with a public opinion that is only one-quarter informed; that, abroad, we are confronted with a public opinion that is widely distrustful of us.

This is the danger: that unless these attitudes are changed, our programs at home and abroad are likely to be defeated and the consequences may be incalculably grave. For this is cold war, this is a vast struggle for men's minds, and it must be waged with full understanding and with full vigor.

The Chinese word for crisis is a combination of two symbols: one is the symbol of opportunity, the other the symbol of disaster. In this great crisis of history, will we realize the opportunity or will we bring on the disaster? What we think, what others think of us, will be the decisive factors in determining the answer.

* * *

In the preceding chapters there have been posed the large problems that confront us in these opinion operations, and there have been suggested some possible approaches toward solving those problems.

This chapter is an attempt to summarize conclusions;

to make some recommendations, necessarily tentative, for bringing about a better informed public opinion; and to point up some of the fundamental issues underlying the whole discussion, notably the issue of leadership.

In stating the problems (in the Introduction) three large areas for action were indicated; similarly the suggestions for possible solutions can be grouped under three heads: first, *the task of education;* second, *the task of implementation;* and, third, *the task of coordination.*

1. The Task of Education

There is, first of all, the need of convincing the government and the people that the public opinion operation is vital.

There are important persons in Washington, officials and high advisers to officials, who will tell you that words are like any other commodity and should be dealt with accordingly. Just as the Department of Commerce handles steel or the Department of Agriculture wheat, in the usual course of business, so the Department of State or the White House should handle words without any special attention.

These important persons are, I think, wrong. Words are an extraordinary commodity, not easy of definition and elusive to handle. Moreover, as this book has tried to demonstrate, they can be used as weapons; their potentialities for both destructive and constructive purposes must, therefore, be realized.

These same persons will tell you, as a corollary, that the public opinion operation is one that is quite incidental to the other activities of the government. Moreover, some of them will contend that the operation is really not a proper function of government but one for private industry and that government ought to quit it as soon as possible.

These opinions, it seems to me, are based on dangerous miscalculations. In the first place, the war of ideology is not over; it is likely to continue so long as the Communists persist in the belief that capitalism is doomed and that, in an attempt to save itself, it will provoke World War III. To abandon our propaganda efforts at this critical stage would be to throw away, recklessly and illogically, a potent and essential weapon.

Again, these observers fail to realize that there is a continuing job to be done at home. Even on that millennial day when all men are neighbors and at peace with one another, when the Russian menace has vanished for all time, there will still be the need of keeping the nation informed. Unless the people know, democracy cannot flourish.

For these reasons an information-propaganda-cultural program will be essential to us for as many years ahead as we can foresee. We ought to recognize its importance and strive to build it boldly and powerfully.

That means that we must get over our fear of the word propaganda; that the Executive shall give to the opinion operation the full measure of attention it deserves; that the Congress shall cooperate, without reservation, in the effort; and that the nation shall expect—and, more than that, demand—the information without which a sound public opinion cannot exist.

Inherent in this discussion is one of those which-comes-first problems. *Item I:* If we have a sound policy and if we do a better job of explaining it, then we shall have a better informed public opinion. *Item II:* If we have a better informed public opinion, the task of evolving a sound foreign policy will be greatly simplified. But there is no point in trying to decide which item has, or should have, precedence. Each derives from and depends on the other, and the efforts to achieve both should proceed simultaneously.

This much is certain: If we had a more enlightened public opinion we would not have to use the shock technique to which the government believes it has to resort to awaken the Congress to the need for a Truman Doctrine or a Marshall Plan or a defense program. These tactics are likely to create a kind of hysteria in the country—a hysteria which may do considerable damage to our sanity at home, especially in the area of civil rights, and to our prestige abroad. Moreover, Congress may eventually develop immunity to shock if this treatment is used too often. The only safe methods for the long run are information and persuasion.

2. The Task of Implementation

The implementation of the opinion operation today is half-hearted and haphazard. The doubts and inertia responsible for such half-heartedness must be dissipated, and unstinted support given to the program. There must be concerted effort by the four branches of the government primarily concerned—the Executive, the Congress, the State and Defense Departments. And private enterprise, notably the press, must do its part and assume its full responsibility.

The role played by Congress is pivotal. Through its power of the purse it can make or break any public opinion program, or shape it according to its own concepts (which are not always enlightened ones). It is urgent, therefore, that Congress have full understanding of the problem. It must be more generous and less caviling in its appropriations for the opinion operation; it should realize that niggardliness in the granting of funds for these programs has led only to ineffectiveness and inefficiency.

Congress should recognize that in this kind of complex operation personnel of the highest order are needed and that good men, impelled as they may be by a desire to do a public service, will not subject themselves to the battering and billingsgate which some members of Congress have leveled at the government's information officials.

In brief, Congress should realize that this is no picayune skirmish in which we are engaged but a campaign of worldwide proportions. Pivotal also is the role of the people. We must learn to recognize the importance of the government's opinion operations and persuade or prod reluctant Congressmen to support them.

Basically, under the present program, the opinion operation at home as well as abroad is a State Department function. Both phases of that operation—intelligence and information—should be extended and improved.

The Government Operation at Home

The task of gauging public opinion at home, the intelligence job, is obviously a difficult one. Yet it must be undertaken because, unless the government is aware of the limits to which the nation will go and is informed about the areas of ignorance it must penetrate, it cannot move with assurance of success in foreign policy. A start has been made, but it is only a start. A much greater effort is needed, in extension of the operation, in refinement of method and especially in enlargement of staff. (The last is, obviously, the important factor and here, again, it is up to Congress.)

With regard to the information process at home there are grave faults which cannot be attributed to Congress but which are due entirely to the Department's failure to correct them. Among the outstanding examples have been these: the briefing of the press has taken place on an uncertain and unsatisfactory basis; the essential task of interpretation of the news has been done on a highly irregular schedule, and not as effectively as it should be; and, particularly, there has been a failure to coordinate the information sources. The remedies for such defects are neither difficult nor drastic; they involve only recognition of the need and determination to push through the reforms, regardless of personalities and protocol.

We should not underestimate the difficulties and the intricacies of the task that confronts the State Department in these operations. Dealing with the American people often requires diplomatic tightrope walking more delicate even than dealing with Russia. As Secretary Acheson has put it:

> If we have a program for giving out information, we are propagandizing. If we don't give out information promptly and system-

atically we are cynically denying your right as citizens to know what is going on behind those musty old walls. Servicing the public with facts is apparently a dangerous business. The Department is damned if it does and it's damned if it doesn't.[1]

Yet, conceding all the difficulties, the main point should be kept firmly in mind: that it is vital at all times to supply a maximum of information to the nation so that it will understand and give foreign policy the support it must have. Surely some of the white-shuttered doors can come down.

The Government Operation Abroad

Difficulties of the same nature confront the government in the opinion operation abroad—difficulties of approach, of method, of personnel. Again there is the division into the intelligence function and the information function.

The intelligence operation abroad should be completely overhauled. That operation holds a great importance for us because, unless we are well informed about what other nations are thinking of us, we cannot fashion policy intelligently. Yet we try to do the job abroad with half a staff; moreover, that half staff is hardly equipped to do that job.

As for the information-propaganda operation abroad, new studies and new approaches seem to be indicated.

The government's long-term programs can well be stepped up. The impression much of the world has of America is one compounded of the Kremlin's portrait of us, of deep prejudices and of false images created by some of our private media. That impression can be corrected only by time and patient endeavor. We must do a better self-portrait; we must emphasize our spiritual aspirations above our material achievements. We must build up our libraries of information. We must further encourage the exchange of teachers and students. We must wholeheartedly support such enterprises as United Nations Educational, Scientific, and Cultural Organization.

[1] Remarks of Dean Acheson at Carnegie Endowment Conference, Nov. 27, 1945, State Department Press Release.

In the short-term program, the Voice of America has had the most attention, but its importance should not be overestimated. In a way, the name "Voice of America" is a misnomer, because there is not really one voice; the United States speaks to Europe with various voices and, more than that, with deeds.

These other voices and these deeds should have the attention they require and deserve. Yet, on the other hand, the importance of the Voice of America should not be underestimated. It can be a powerful force in influencing opinion abroad if it is properly scripted and if medium and long wave are used in place of short wave so that the number of potential listeners is greatly increased. Here, too, it is largely a question of funds.

The other important aspect of the short-range operation is the provision of official statements and news for press and radio stations abroad. The theory has been advanced that the government should not engage in a news operation because the news will be suspect as propaganda, even though the word propaganda is used in its best and most benevolent sense; and that, therefore, all news operations should be left to the private news agencies.

They should be, so far as possible, but in the areas into which the news agencies do not and cannot reach, the government must undertake the assignment. Certainly in these areas, until private enterprise can take over the job, government must attempt to supply our side of the arguments and an un-Cominform version of the news.[2]

The Task of Private Enterprise

Private enterprise should play a larger and more responsible part in the foreign operation.

[2] This point was made strongly by the Hutchins Commission. "We also recommend that, where the private agencies of mass communication are unable or unwilling to supply information about this country to a particular foreign country or countries, the government employ mass communication media of its own to supplement this deficiency." See *A Free and Responsible Press, op. cit.,* p. 89.

Of first importance is private enterprise's role in the dissemination of news. There is a great opportunity for bringing about an understanding among democratic nations through the minds of the editors. The American news agencies sell their services to numerous newspapers abroad. They would do well, however, to make certain that the news they supply fairly represents this country. If the editors abroad understand us, we shall have achieved a great propaganda gain. One wonders whether it would not be extremely valuable if there were set up a World Press Institute, modeled after the American Press Institute,[3] to which editors from all parts of the world would come to discuss both the theory and practice of journalism.

The motion picture industry and all our other media of mass communication likewise have a great responsibility. They, too, ought to realize that the nature of the foreign operation is different from that of the domestic; that their function is not entertainment alone, or even entertainment; that though these are private enterprises, they are endowed, so far as the foreign field is concerned, with a kind of ambassadorial quality. And their performance should be guided by that responsibility.

3. The Task of Coordination

There are times when the cynic, surveying such episodes as the Palestine and Smith-Molotov affairs, is inclined to lump together all the government's information agencies into a Babel Department. So many are the voices speaking to this nation and to other nations, and so varied are the tongues! So often do we hear conflicting statements about the course we are following or should be following abroad! No wonder, despite all the planning committees, despite all the reorganizations, despite bipartisan foreign policies, the American public is confused.

---

[3] This Institute meets at Columbia University each year for a series of sessions that have brought about a better understanding among the editors of the country and a better technique of journalism.

If public support of our foreign policy is to be attained, it is not enough to perfect the individual agencies; it is essential also that there be thorough coordination among these agencies, and inside each of them. Above all, there must be assurance that they are all following the same policy and conforming to the information programs devised to implement that policy.

Within the State Department, this means that coordination between the officials of the geographic offices and of the information bureaus must be improved, at all levels, and that greater efforts should be made to bring about the participation of the information men in the informal as well as the formal policy-making structure of the Department.

Coordination among the departments is a much larger and more complicated endeavor, because it involves so many agencies, so many officials (many of them in the highest brackets), so much "face" and so much protocol. Foreign policy is comparable to the assembling of a watch, so delicate is the mechanism and so many are the parts; it is inconceivable that you would summon twenty or forty watchmakers to do the final assembly job on a single timepiece, and yet at times that is what we try to do in foreign policy.

Coordination must start with the relations between the White House and the State Department. Obviously the liaison between the President and the Secretary has to be very close, so that there will be agreement in the content of policy and in its timing. Yet, unless the President is his own Secretary of State, as Roosevelt in effect was, the link seems to have weakened; the removal of the Department from its historic building across the street from the White House to a site a mile away has been almost symbolic.

Because in the present cold war, or hot truce, military potential weighs heavily, it is obvious that the State and Defense Departments have to work closely together, both in the formulation of policy and in the explanation of that policy to the country. The guiding hand ought to be that of State and that hand should not be forced by Defense.

Most difficult and baffling of all are the relations between Congress and the State Department; unless they are good, and unless the Congress agrees with the general objectives sought abroad by the Executive, we present to the world a picture of divided counsels that is a number one item for the Russian propaganda machine.

Congress will have to learn to be more sophisticated about our foreign affairs and more sympathetic with those who manage them. And there is no question that the State Department can make a larger contribution to harmony. More frequent conferences between Congressional leaders and Department officials, the furnishing of fuller information to Congressmen and the maintenance of an able group of expert advisers to Congressional committees are all devices that will serve to improve the Department's relations with Capitol Hill and thus to promote a more unified foreign policy.

The coordination of our propaganda efforts overseas is also essential; otherwise there will be a loss of effectiveness and a confusion among the editors and others in the information field with whom we are required to deal abroad.

There should be more communication between our diplomatic representatives in foreign lands and the Department's information bureaus. The diplomats, who are on the spot and who should, presumably, be able to sense the temper in their areas, should offer suggestions for lines of propaganda policy and ideas for propaganda programs.

4. *The Key Figure: The Coordinator*

The one point that should be made above all in this discussion of State Department coordination is this: that a coordinator of all the opinion operations in the Department is essential—a coordinator with ample authority and ample elbow-room.

It has been said repeatedly in this book that the importance of the opinion operation has not been realized in the government and that it must be. It is said again here because it has so direct a bearing on this question of the coordinator.

The force of public opinion must be recognized, both in the formation of policy and in the explanation and promotion of policy. Unless the probable impact of an international move, on the thoughts and attitudes of the American people and on peoples abroad, is weighed when that move is in the planning stage, one of the vital factors will have been left out of account and failure may result. Unless a full effort is made to explain the move to the nation and the world, our motives may well be questioned and our purpose defeated.

There are, then, two functions involved: policy making (which calls for good intelligence) and policy explaining (which calls for good information). The policy-explaining function has been implemented in some degree. The policy-making function, as it applies to opinion, has had too little attention.

The two functions are different but they are definitely related; moreover, the same expert knowledge and wisdom are needed for both. Therefore, there should be—presumably in the Department—a single, highly paid official who would be, in effect, the head of a public opinion desk. He would be in charge both of the information operation at home and of the information-propaganda operation abroad.

This official would sit in with the policy-making group of the Department and would play an important part in its deliberations; thus, he could help form policy and acquire the knowledge needed to explain policy adequately. The opposite of an official censor, he would see that both current and background information with regard to our foreign affairs would be made available as soon as possible and in the most effective manner. He would try to loosen up the tight-lipped career men but, at the same time, he would guard against leaks which might endanger our diplomatic relations. It is a job of vast importance and difficult to fill, but it is one that is vital to any foreign policy program.

There are those who suggest that the public opinion operation with regard to foreign policy should be taken from the State Department and handled by an independent agency. In the belief of this observer, it should stay in the State Department if only for this reason: full attention must be given to public opinion in the formation of foreign policy.

At this point two disavowals are set down emphatically. In the first place it is not proposed to set up an omnipotent Ministry of Propaganda which might at some time dedicate itself to the cause of a Fuehrer or a Sacred State. In the second place it is not even suggested that the coordinator of public information shall be either a poll expert or a press agent. His is the task of analyzing and synthesizing public opinion, so that he can inform the government, so far as it is possible, as to what the nation is thinking, not for the purpose that public opinion shall be followed unquestioningly, but for the purpose that the grave problems of opinion shall be better understood.

5. *The Tough Question of Leadership*

Thus far in this book the question of leadership has been raised only as incidental to other issues. Yet it is a fundamental element in the problem which is the theme of this book.

These are days when leadership is sorely needed to bring light into the dark areas of ignorance and the darker areas of prejudice; and to state and restate some of the great truths the nation must come to accept as axioms.

We must learn the full fallacy of concepts such as these: that isolation is still possible for us; that foreigners are inevitably aliens and cannot be genuine allies; that help for other nations is charity and not help for ourselves; that we can sell without buying; that we can have prosperity in a stricken world.

We must learn to keep always in mind basic beliefs such as these: that a community of nations is essential to us; that spiritual values are greater than material; that ideas can never be conquered with arms but only with truths; that Communism cannot be obliterated with atom bombs but only through economic betterment; above all, that aggressive war must be forever held to be a crime and that we must unhesitatingly move against it.

In any official opinion program the President's role is the prime factor. His is the Voice of the Nation at home and his is the Voice of America abroad. If that voice speaks in halting or uncertain tones, the program is hopelessly crippled; if the President fails to assert leadership, no matter how great the effort of the State Department or any of the other agencies, our objectives will not be attained. The President, then, must speak out vigorously for our way of life at home and for our role abroad. Democracy must step up its broadcasts.

The leader—be he President or Secretary of State or Congressman—must hear the voice of the people and he must heed it, but if he is really a leader he will direct it also. For a leader must lead, he must not follow or be pushed onward from behind. He must decide what is, according to his best judgment, the right course and he must follow that course, regardless of what the polls may reveal or what the commentators may shout.

On the other hand, leadership must be realistic. The leader must be able to gauge the distance he can safely go; if he moves too far ahead he loses touch with his followers, he becomes a voice crying in the wilderness and one that will soon fade out. The wisdom of this precept is seen clearly in the contrast between Wilson's course with the League of Nations issue and Roosevelt's in the early days of the Hitler threat.

Wilson was greatly and indubitably right in principle; but he was wrong in his failure to take sufficient note of the state of opinion. If, in the light of the warnings, he had compromised, he might have had not a perfect League but a useful one, rather than a League that turned out, because of our abstention, to be none—and this, in turn, might have changed the course of history in the twenties and thirties and so possibly have helped to avert World War II.

In 1937 Roosevelt made his famous Quarantine speech, warning the Fascist nations against going too far. But the country was not yet ready and it indicated that dissent in emphatic terms. Roosevelt took note of the opinion semaphores and slowed his pace. He began to move more cautiously and thus more effectively, but he never swerved from his course. Then came the destroyer deal, the extraordinary device of lend-lease and the other measures of help for the opponents of Hitler; and all the while he was educating the country away from isolationism.

Those episodes out of recent history indicate clearly the importance of taking the opinion factor into full account. They illuminate what the relationship should be between the coordinator of public information and the President or any of the other policy makers—to appraise opinion for guidance in policy making; to acquire information for use in policy explaining; to collect intelligence for direction in propaganda.

6. The Basic Element: A Sound Policy

Let us understand what we are here advocating. Call it information or call it propaganda, it is education on a vast scale. We have been discussing what the government can contribute to that end.

But it is emphasized again here that government alone cannot perform the task of education required in the kind of world into which we have been thrust—or even a large part of that task. That is an effort—almost a crusade—in which all the forces of potential illumination must unite—the schools, the press, the instruments of adult education, as well as the government.

On the other hand, we must not minimize the government's part in the operation. It is the government that has the final responsibility for drafting policy. It is the government that decides what the people shall know. It is the government that must supply the leadership.

But education and leadership will fail unless the basic element is good: policy must be sound. We must have a foreign policy that will win the support of an enlightened public at home and convince peoples abroad that our motives are good. That policy must be candid without being naive, realistic yet sympathetic, formed and yet flexible. Above all, it must be built on understanding—on our understanding of ourselves, on our understanding of others, on others' understanding of us.

Such a policy is not easily made. It cannot be produced out of a crucible in a laboratory, nor by a group of experts in an ivory tower, nor by pollsters probing the public brain in the highways and byways. It must be the result of the meeting of many minds after the distillation of many reports.

That policy cannot be stiff, or formal or statistical; it must be human. The European Recovery Program is built on masses of figures and estimates; yet when all the multiplication and all the division are done, all the mathematics completed, the big decisions will be made according to hunches. It is the intangibles in any international problem that really carry weight. Of these intangibles public opinion ranks almost first, in range and in difficulty of appraisal.

"One person with a belief," wrote John Stuart Mill, "is a social power equal to ninety-nine who have only interests." We must believe in ourselves and in our cause. We must persuade others of our steadfast purpose, of our national unity, of our fundamental sincerity. Ours is an information-propaganda task of huge proportions; it cannot be accomplished unless it is undertaken with truth and with conviction, for these, of all tools, are still the most powerful.